Broken and Reset

Mary Burritt
Christiansen
Poetry Series

Mary Burritt Christiansen
Poetry Series

V. B. Price, *Series Editor*

*Also available in the
University of New Mexico Press
Mary Burritt Christiansen
Poetry Series*

Poets of the Non-Existent City:
Los Angeles in the McCarthy Era
edited by Estelle Gershgoren Novak

Selected Poems of Gabriela Mistral
edited by Ursula K. Le Guin

Deeply Dug In by R. L. Barth

Amulet Songs: Poems Selected and New
by Lucile Adler

In Company: An Anthology of
New Mexico Poets After 1960
edited by Lee Bartlett, V. B. Price,
and Dianne Edenfield Edwards

Tiempos Lejanos: Poetic Images from the Past
by Nasario García

Refuge of Whirling Light
by Mary Beath

The River Is Wide/El río es ancho:
Twenty Mexican Poets, a Bilingual Anthology
edited and translated by Marlon L. Fick

A Scar Upon our Voice by Robin Coffee

CrashBoomLove: A Novel in Verse
by Juan Felipe Herrera

Rebirth of Wonder: Poems of the Common Life
by David Johnson

In a Dybbuk's Raincoat: Collected Poems
by Bert Meyers
edited by Morton Marcus and Daniel Meyers

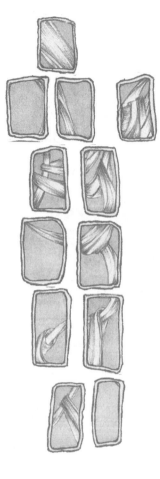

broken
and reset

Selected Poems

1966 to 2006

V. B. Price

UNIVERSITY OF NEW MEXICO PRESS

ALBUQUERQUE

© 2007 by the University of New Mexico Press
All rights reserved. Published 2007
Printed in the United States of America
12 11 10 09 08 07   1 2 3 4 5 6 7

Library of Congress Cataloging-in-Publication Data

Price, V. B. (Vincent Barrett)
Broken and reset : selected poems,
1966 to 2006 / V.B. Price.
p. cm. — (Mary Burritt Christiansen poetry series)
ISBN 978-0-8263-4157-0 (alk. paper)
I. Title.
PS3566.R548B76 2007
811'.54—DC22

                    2007009474

DESIGN AND COMPOSITION: *Mina Yamashita*

For Rini, as always, and our wonderful, far flung family

In Memoriam

Edith Barrett Price
Vincent L. Price Jr.
Marjorie H. Rini
Mary Grant Price
Anne Seymour
Helen K. Herman
S. Jack Rini
Rosalie Buddington
Sandra Rae Greenwald
James Michael Jenkinson
Patrick Chester Henderson
Roland Francis Dickey
Rosalie Buddington
Mark Douglas Acuff
Katherine G. Simons
George Clayton Pearl
Lucile Adler
Cecil Robert Lloyd

There is more than one world and more than one set of virtues.
*   —Isaiah Berlin, The Originality of Machiavelli*

. . . some have taught that the bees have received a share of the divine
intelligence, and a draught of heavenly ether; for God, they say,
pervades all things, earth and seas' expanse and heaven's depth.
*   —Virgil, Georgics*

That our senses lie and our minds trick us is true, but in general
They are honest Rustics; trust them a little;
The senses more than the mind, and your own mind more than
another man's.
*   —Robinson Jeffers, "Advice to Pilgrims"*

contents

Acknowledgments

My thanks and appreciation go to the editors and publishers of *The Southwest Review, Manhattan Review, dust, Beloit Poetry Journal, Seared Eye, Goliards, Encanto, Albierto Quarterly, discourse, New York Quarterly, Contents Under Pressure, Wild Dog, New Mexico Independent, South Dakota Review, Today, Sunstone Review, Uzzano, Calliope, Images, Century, Connecticut Quarterly, Occident, El Palacio, Skull Polish, Confrontation, Artspace, Puerto del Sol, Tarasque, Alpha Beat Press, Lucid Moon, Lucid Stone, Cold Mountain Review, Clockwork Review, Galley Sail Review, Washout, Serpent's Egg, St. Elizabeth Street, Back Door, Very Special Arts New Mexico, New Mexico Magazine,* and *Telepoem.*

I owe special thanks to the late Roland Dickey, editor of *New Mexico Quarterly* and former director of UNM Press, and to Mary Adams, assistant editor of *New Mexico Quarterly* for first publishing me in 1962 and mentoring me for decades. Katherine Simons, master teacher and Shakespeare scholar at the University of New Mexico, encouraged me and led me to believe I was worth my best efforts. John R. Milton, editor of the *South Dakota Review,* published my longer poems for over two decades, never failing to encourage me. Luther Wilson, director of UNM Press, has given me the opportunity to edit the Mary Burritt Christensen Poetry Series, and has backed me consistently in many projects that would not have come into existence without his support. Beth Hadas, former director of UNM Press, has been a wise guide and constant friend for many years. Don and Pamela Michaelis of *Wingspread Collector's Guide* published an ambitious four-color collaboration between artist Rini Price and myself called *Death Self;* we are forever grateful. Bill Peterson, of Artspace

Press, gave photographer Kirk Gittings and myself the opportunity to publish "Chaco Body" in a beautifully designed edition. Bill gave of himself for decades to New Mexico's artists. Kirk made the Chaco Body poems possible by proposing and supporting our collaboration. J. B. Bryan, publisher of La Alameda Press, has been a blessing for years to many New Mexico poets, myself included. Jennifer Bartlett and Jim Stewart of St. Elizabeth Street Press in Brooklyn, New York, published my modern sequel to the Homeric Hymns called *Myth Waking*, taking a risk with their new enterprise. Marsha Muth and the editors of Sunstone Press and E. W. Tedlock of San Marcos Press backed me from the start. As with so many New Mexico poets, Ward Abbott, poet, bookseller, and publisher, allowed many experimental works of mine to see print. I'm grateful for the generosity and editing of Miriam Sagan and Sharon Niederman for including me in their anthology *New Mexico Poetry Renaissance* published by Red Crane Press, and editors Jeanie C. Williams and Victor di Suvero who produced at Pennywhistle Press the anthology *Saludos: Poemas de Nuevo Mexico*. And I give my thanks and admiration to Elise M. McHugh, the production editor of this book, for her wisdom and generous care.

I have been blessed with the friendship of many poets, writers, architects, artists, musicians, readers, and kin, all of whom have kept me going. They include my core readers, the people who get every poem I write: Skip and Gloria Graham, Mary Beath, Denise Clegg, Michaela Renz, John Cordova, Chris and Buff Hungerland, Don and Pamela Michaelis, Lee Lyon, Jim Rini, and Jackie Niccoli. I am grateful always for family readers: Jody Price, Keir Price, Victoria Price, Jacki Fuqua, Chris Fuqua, and Marc Fuqua. And my friends have been indispensable: David Johnson, Lucile Adler, Winfield Townley Scott, J. B. Bryan, Ward Abbott, Charles Tomlinson, Witter Bynner, Lee Bartlett, Jennifer Bartlett and Jim Stewart, Cecil Robert Lloyd, Dianne Edwards, Toad House, Richard Hogan, Craig Watson, Marc Simmons, Baker Morrow, Danny Crafts, Lynne Reeve, Francis Roe, Elizabeth Wolf, Lynn and Charlie Bieble, Kirk Gittings, Eleni Bastea, Sharon Niederman, Tom Harmon, Jack Ehn, Robert George, Sally Sanstchi, James Michael Jenkinson, Patrick Henderson, Polly Summar, Ralph Looney, Mildred Gifford, George Clayton Pearl, Mark Acuff, Mary Beth Acuff, Chris Wilson, Mike Thomas, Leslie Donovan, Charles Poling, Richard Fox, Milas Hurley, Sue Vorenberg, and Daniel Abraham.

I owe special thanks to Charles Bieble and Rosalie Otero, former and current directors of the University of New Mexico University Honors Program, who have given me more than twenty years of the sheer joy of thinking with young people in interdisciplinary seminars in the classics, poetry, contemporary issues, the U.S. Constitution, and other topics.

As with everything I've done since 1968, my deepest love and gratitude go to my wife, the artist Rini Price, my first reader, first editor, and most trusted friend and critic.

Introduction

Broken and Reset is a selection of poems written over the last forty years while I was making my living as a reporter, columnist, nonfiction writer, editor, novelist, and teacher. Both making poems and making a living have allowed me to pursue my real occupation of trying to repair my ignorance. I'm a working-class writer and partial autodidact who was saved from a life of sordid tedium, and maybe even madness and crime, by believing I could evolve from my feral childhood and civilize myself by learning to read, write, and think. This basic faith in learning came to me from the progressive and pragmatic heart of American culture. Luck has been my friend too. I was given a choice to move to New Mexico to go to school when I was eighteen. And I took it. I can't imagine who I would be if I hadn't.

I studied anthropology, English, and philosophy and literature at the University of New Mexico, and realized that even though I would always be unprepared to be a formal scholar, I could become a collector—of ideas, of information about how the world works, of other people's writing, of rocks, shells, history, books and art, and of the kind of experience that only poetry and reporting, and reading where your curiosity takes you, can offer.

I won't glorify my standoffishness by calling myself an outsider, but I am a stubborn character, antisocial when it comes to being influenced, eccentric in the sense of needing to be utterly free (while well disguised in normalcy), and a believer in the ordinary genius of everyone. The great learning experiences of my life have come to me from my dissatisfaction with being in the dark, with not having read and studied what I assumed every well-educated person should have, and from my interest in the history, natural environment, and cultures of New Mexico. Like most autodidacts, I am friend-taught, learning almost as much from conversation as from reading. Always a late bloomer, when I was given the chance to teach in the University of New Mexico Honors program in 1986, my learning curve accelerated as it never had before. I discovered Hermes and Odysseus again as an adult. I was instructed by Thucydides in the corruption of power and given hope by Artemis and Aphrodite. I became interested in politics as a teenager because Aldous Huxley and George Orwell made it clear to me that free people are constantly in danger of being gulled by political predators who prey on our weaknesses, laziness, and fear. Poetry attracted me then, as well, because it seemed fearless and at odds with authority. And even though I wasn't sure what a metaphor was, I think I could sense, without the words to describe it, that poets could help me heal myself as a stutterer and panicked recluse. I've always had the impulse to hold strong opinions. I tend to like people who have the same leaning. I've written a newspaper column on politics and the environment every week, sometimes three times a week, since 1971. I have learned more by having to witness the world, and then defend a point of view about it, than I could have learned any other way.

The title *Broken and Reset* comes from not only being lucky enough to have escaped the crippling traps of my childhood but also the decadent mainstream of modern America and the conformity that in-groups and gatekeepers require. The fractures of my early life didn't heal properly in Los Angeles where I was raised. I had to break the faulty mends and reset them in New Mexico. I dreamed myself up in Albuquerque. I found language to be the perfect instrument for me to practice. And I have, from time to time, felt Orpheus's shadow pass across the page, allowing me to see intimations of my better self.

—V. B. Price, Albuquerque, New Mexico

later

poems

2006–1995

The High Alone

I. Albuquerque

Adventures begin.
What is
is perfectly what is.
Nothing can ever go wrong.
Wrong
requires standards
outside what is.
And there is
nothing
outside what is.
It is all and nothing;
that's the gift
of freedom in its purity.
Fear alone makes the difference,
draws the line
across the universe—
fear the great savior
with so little to do,
it just keeps running
and running,

winding and winding, until
it snaps
with a fatal lash
across our tenderness.
But even it
isn't wrong.
Even the idea of wrong
isn't wrong.
So, what is?
Are we wrong-headed
seeing wrong
in what displeases us,
or wants to eat us?
What's to be done?
Just begin.

II. Ouray

In the deep covers
in the box canyon,
in the far corner
of the world of dawn,
I twist myself
into a knotty sweat, wrinkled
in egos, politics,
and names in their chains
on the burning ladders
of it-hurts-so-much-
for-so-little successes,
and then, bored
with the broken chorus of angels, dusty with
torment,
singing the same six notes of sad,
my wiser self

whispered through that slumbering fret
"You can imagine
anything you want,
you know." And I
instantly unbound,
safe in loose pajamas,
flannel robe and carpet slippers,
delicious
kitchen warmth
soothing the true
critter me I'd become
with the gorgeous idea of morning.
We both fell asleep,
my wise self and I,
and we have both
woken up in the same
nightshirt this morning.

III. Meeker

The world is spinning, puking,
falling out of chairs;
people are murdering each other,
mothers are bathing their children,
others are bathing corpses,
and the lucky ones
pick our way among
rows of wilted land mines,
spiked with live ones,
with no help, no trauma.
Only the news for us makes it seem
the slaughter of the innocents
won't shut up.
Seeming is believing.
But the truth is much
worse than it seems.
The countless well placed of us
are still rushed and sad,
bombarded by wants we don't have,
and features from hell
exploding, sifting their damp
grainy shadows into our soiled
soft heavenly beds.
Is it a duty
or a habit
to keep swimming
to the end,
hoping for one
last pocket of air?

IV. Laramie

Beethoven grass
teasing and rolling
through the high alone,
surrounding us
with inner spaces
as far as we can breathe, intimate
as not being seen, as soul mates
conversing over supper,
rising and falling with each other, fitting perfectly
as geology and weather,
as bone and the chemistry of ideas.
Politics is seen for what it is
—death house green
gas storage tanks and pipelines,
fiscal zits defined benign
by those making money
for themselves
from what belongs to all of us,
wanting to steal that future
rising in us
as our whole true being with each other
under the sky. Among the notes
swelling across the plains,
money is just
ticks and lice in the beautiful
fur of the music
bounding over the hills.

V. Glenwood Springs

Ego leather,
old gloves
tough, soft
with use
as when
you stop
comparing who you are
to others, greedy
for more
from yourself,
wanting praise
from those
who mean nothing.
Then ego becomes
an old shovel,
sanded, filed down to an edge,
with histories of dozens of gardens in it,
then it becomes
the other face of the guide you can trust
but only
when it compares
who you are
to who you really are
with just
a little more
patience.

VI. Durango

Tangles of rushing,
the mess of the times
turning the briar paths
of achievement into jumbles
of junked derricks,
winches, oily chains and old
motels shipwrecked with only
the tattered signs of what
havens they once were in storms, all now just
dumped down
speculations.
Only wind tides on the land,
pronghorns surfing currents,
riding grass swells with their muscles,
can advise us.
If we could live
in motion, honest
to our natures, even in
mires of needs and time,
without ambition but to flow,
we could finally say
we've learned how
to move like a blade
not a fist,
like a breath
not an anvil
falling from the 55th floor.

VII. Albuquerque

Beginning is always.
Who you were
is not
who you are, anymore than you are
your name,
your aches and pains,
your failures,
your grand accolades.
As beginning is
forever, all ending
is a crease in the carpet,
bunched up time,
messed matter settling,
always leveling
and rolling up
greater than
flatness.

What matters
is starting, always,
always again
the fathomless chance
to get it right,
to follow the cracked leaves, bent twigs,
flutters of red string
through the forest,
zeroing in
on beginning
as it flows always
toward its freedom, always
with you and without you,
beyond hope, beyond virtue,
beyond reward. ∎

Orpheus the Healer

I. As Good an Instrument as You Can Make

A nerve
    misfiring
in the center of your brain,
    separation
    stops
    and disappears
once you hear your own voice
    make meaning
    that's beyond you,
a voice you'd swear was yours,
    a gorgeous squawking
    on a tin can violin,
or playing itself on your green twig piano
    as it joy-odes
    through your rasping.

That voice
is you
     and not
      who you are.
So how can you be apart,
     broken out
     from the divine,
when Orpheus sings through you,
even when your vocal cords
break apart like rubber bands too long in the sun?
     All that matters
      is being played,
       is hearing the voice
come from your pen
without
you thinking
a thing.

II. Cleansing

Healed of being human
                              only,
only a graft,
not the full tree,
        just the intrusion
        above the cut,
              the artificial part, rootless
                                    on the tree of life,
you are free
when Orpheus allows
        the jungle to grow up
        through you
and you understand why
the divine has led you on
        past the squeaking of your reason,
on
to the full, teeming joy
                          of the music of nothing.
The divine,
how it loves
        the big cats, novas, sequoias,
        the mugwort and the algae,
        how it loves to slum around
                                thinking
with our minds
or speed along with the calm of snails
        following their shiny trails,
                              like poems
                              leave
                              our traces.

III. Cloudless

Stuffed headed
clown ego
    gets its rest
    when Orpheus sings through you
so cleanly and with such
    a gorgeous instinct
    for the sublime,
that even pride
refuses,
out of self-respect,
to claim it,
    ashamed to cheat,
    to trade upon the gifting.
No vanity is possible,
no identity derived
    when all you've done
    is practice,
tilling a dry field until
an Orphic storm
or drizzle
    flowers up
    the mysteries
in the furrow mazes
of your half
filled container.

IV. Body of Song

How can body and mind
    be denied
    each other
when Orpheus wants to dance
      with darling Logos
through the lightning
    waters of the brain?
We can't know
    anything,
    can we,
but the feel
of how
    words mean to us
      bodily
      among the packets of atoms.
Orpheus is
as flesh is
an element.
He sang in Hell
    to make skin and bones again
    of his one desire,
    that woman,
      wanted, like a sail
        of nerves
        is wanted,
      by the far
      sea breathing
      of Eros as he sings
—even Orpheus
    welcomes a greater god
    to fill him to the brim
and over.

V. One, All, Forever

Metaphors are facts.
Is this the lesson of the lyre?
Oceanic forests,
    swaying tides,
poems
pulling data
    into turbulence
    so rich and safe
        trees dance
        with rocks and grass,
        and lions read
             the comets;
       each of us,
       as we are,
       moments
       of a universe in which
    gods and pain, dust, hips, warm clean hands,
    meadows, dark woods, the curvature of space,
    apologies and ice, midwives, warriors,
    and perfect ears of corn,
are all
of the same
improbability,
    all real and realized
    like poems
    flowing from time,
    the invisible plain
    of what always is
    just next.

VI. No Moral Pollution

Politics and religion vanish
    like dust nebulae
    and wrinkled jokes
when Orpheus is
at high tide in us.
His Voice cures us
    of our suspicion
        that sins, even momentary
        lapses and mistakes,
    mean more than mental bumps,
are taints, in fact,
never to be removed.
He cures us of our simple,
stupid absolutes.
    I loathe Stalin. Neruda, for a time, did not.
I love Neruda, despite the Soviet,
    and pledge my fealty, like him,
    to the working body,
    the working life,
    the body of work
    that injustice
    rarely overlooks.

Rumi is the guide of guides
to fields beyond false boundaries,
though I feel
    that Islam, Judaism, Christianity, *Das Kapital* and the *Wealth of Nations*
are made of iron bars
    bent all the time into chains
    by thugs and morons
        who believe
        in nothing
and for whom
Orpheus would be
a devil in me
    and worth my life
to extract him
if they knew he was there
waiting to cure
their stainless steel hearts
    with the trust of a sparrow
    resting in his hand.

VII. Just Is

Orpheus,
you know how it is
to be almost a god,
      except for your need.
The god in you
      does nothing,
      which is everything we want.
The music of the spheres and cells, of all things everywhere
wells up in you
           . . . but
for imposing the force of desire. . . .
      All that intentional doing
      is the error
      that it leads to,
        the final death of what you want.
She was not
an instrument
for you to play,
already radiant as she was
with death's empty light,
      the way death is its own
     effortless not doing.

Song flows out of you like that,
     like exhalation,
     god-almost,
     the rest, the trying, the longing
     is torn apart and scattered,
     and what is left
     sings on
          in each of us
          distinctly
          as our snoring,
               our kissing, laughing, sighing, coughing,
          and because of you,
             if we listen,
we can sometimes
tell who we are. ■

Fatal Summer

I. April 29, 2003

Black flowers
not ash or char,
not blood black,
not eyes closed
middle of the brain black,
not inside the
meat locker black,
not bruise black,
not melanoma black,
not death's cowl black,
but flowers black
as pupils drinking light,
not Pluto's blossoms,
the flowering of absence,
but the black
at the edge of now
and the new now
that's always next.

II. August 10, 2003

This death in the family,
this vampire death, divorce, so
virtual, so
dead and still sucking,
this smeared erasure,
I prefer pestilence to it,
torture corsets,
the guilty-doubt clutches
of parent-spouse inquisitors,
regimes of self-purging,
marriages gagging,
lost lust the emetic.
What insanity that "love"
contorts into a doilied,
breakfast-nooked enigma
with its Iron Barbie
pointedly wide open.
Is anyone wise enough
to see it coming—
when death opens wide
the basement door, the steep
stairs of dissent, virtual
or not, leading up
to the hair-trigger smile
the hooded one with the ax
can't keep from smiling?
I smile right back, long gone
out the door, in love
with Freedom's daughter, far, far away
from the squalid
pieties of love's empty tin.

III. August 20, 2003

for George Clayton Pearl

It's not like your corpse,
looking like a gigolo
in your unwanted
sunroof casket,
hair blow dried,
wrinkles
botoxed away,
a pencil line
of mascara
on your upper lip,
it's not like that,
this wiping away
of the nicks and dings
of our years of sparring
and the paper cuts
of hurt feelings.
They're all gone
and what is left for me
is not a
faux ideal,
but a man with bulging knuckles
who sustained a thousand cuts
from his exuberance in doing,
in laboring, in being
a phenomenon of nature,
loving with abandon
its own best nature.

IV. August 21, 2003

We who are left behind
by all our fathers and mothers, we remain
in the world of pleasure and panic,
the world that is lost to them,
the world we love and fear so much,
the world so utterly beyond our control,
the world so incompletely of our own invention and perspective,
the world we can suffer or adore,
detest or savor,
denounce or secretly
and pervasively
conspire to applaud
in complex and deep
complicity
with its beauty
and its companion
—the life and death loyalty
and lonely respect
among those of us still
grieving, reluctantly
waiting to leave.

V. August 24, 2003

The old friend is dead,
his foibles, though profound,
in the smallness of their ways,
matter less than dust
on the pure piano now,
except for his last
indecisions
which shock us
like finding scorpions,
with their stingers roughly removed,
clotted in the sock drawer.
In a dream, I bypass a friend,
in a three stooges hospital caper,
who'd fallen from his gurney
when it collapsed
like a Popeil Pocket
Strategic Satellite.
It's all silly, silly as wearing
a fatal blister on your heel, insisting
on the slippers with the golden buckles
and pointy toes,
and you, therefore, a tiptoeing hippo,
graceless and serenely
foibled to death.
"I sentence you. . . . May many
small fools
have mercy on your soul." ■

from *Myth Waking*
Homeric Hymns, A Modern Sequel

Real faith is "a resting in something that surrounds and holds us," and any anthropomorphizing of it must be done in the deepest unconscious.
　　　　　　　　　　　—Lou Andreas-Salomé

That is always best which gives me to myself.
　　　　　　　　　　　—Ralph Waldo Emerson

... the effective identification with everything, the re-merging with everything [is] ... the positive basic aim of the libido.
　　　　　　　　　　　—Lou Andreas-Salomé

The Muses

Every trust I have
came first through you,
even wisdom beyond experience
—a miracle
for someone so unwise.
It wasn't just
words on pages,
but what the words knew
that I didn't know
that caused me first to trust you,
trust what I couldn't see
before I'd said it.

Open me again.
Every happiness I owe to you,
to where you've taken me
beyond the literal.

Perfume
of perfection,
you even can arouse
drab fumbling
to overflow
and sound the truth;
like the energy of time
that plays us all,
as masters play
the unknown singing of the nerves,
you voice us truly
even if we don't
quite know
what we've said. ■

Eros

Irresistibly
everywhere, fragrant,

nude of doubt, joy soaked, so
like water moving up

through tree flesh
helplessly into air, Eros

draws his hand
to her waist

his fingers lifting, sliding
under the edge

of her shirt,
as they sit,

backs to the world,
at a center table,

sensing no pain
in the dark edges

of their lives. So like
Psyche's light, voluptuous,

magnetized by fact, the lovers
cannot help but reveal

what wants to stay
under the covers. The sexual place

that never sleeps
is mind, after all,

feeling around in the dark
for love. And so

we see every time
that Eros is not

good looks, not
banal sightings

of faultless form,
but Chaos born,

warm blooded,
unformed without

the loving other.
It's not so odd

Eros is a baby
in comic book cosmologies,

not a strange translation
for the purity

of attraction
that can't be made impure,

though Thanatos,
that drain of want,

that irresistible lack,
shadows close enough to be

mistaken for a stain.
Eros alone

is free of ending.
Moon pulled,

tide gorged, indiscriminately
full of purpose,

how could Eros not
be the god

of the petal skin of babies,
and of bodies who when touched

whisper "baby" in your ear?
Numinous, beyond

choice, the eternal yes
that's never out of place,

Eros is so
much of everything

we all want
all the time

that even death
wants to die

like noble
lovers who just

can't stop
for the life of them. ■

Hermes

I.

Hermes, like death,
cannot be said.

He's uncontrollable because
he is ungraspable,

tricky
because he's trusted,

believable
as sudden fame,

dependable
as a gamble

because
he doesn't mind.

His mind
is moonlight,

treacherous
and sublime,

generous
and unconfined.

I've trusted him blind.
I've had to—moon-eyed,

fright-teased, owned
by the habits of others.

He knew the way
to speak my mind.

He let me see
a god's a god

and not much help, except
to be a clue

not to confuse
with yourself.

Hermes, the guide,
makes the difference

when he's on your side.
He *is* your mind,

when it's not
self-deceived,

the god of your best
imperfections,

the trustworthy pattern
that's never the same.

II.

Luminous
and razor gray,

Hermes cures
night blindness

adjusting me
to the spare,

the ambiguous,
the strange.

He finds my way
through orchard canopies,

virgin bowers and caves of shade,
childly wild with me,

a glowing indirection
through the pines.

I trust him
never to succumb

to habit,
never to be

expected
and on time.

Moonlight minded,
slippery as trying

to keep true,
the Death Scout,

doesn't help us
when we want him,

only when we need him,
if we have believed him

when he tricks us
with his truths.

III.

Oh, death is a crowd
so thick

there is no room for us
without the Guide.

Our faces are just masks to us
until he sees us

as we know we are.
He mirrors us

in history
and in luck.

Nothing can outwit him
in the dark.

With him, we thrive
in shadows,

in ripples, cloud wisps,
in waving leaves.

He knows the way out.
He's refused

to choose between
happiness and survival.

He creates the truth he needs,
describes the choice away.

With him, the dangerous
and indefinite become

our easy habitat
beyond suspicion and control

of tyrants who must know
EVERYTHING

to booby-trap
our trust

in the ice of floodlights
night blinded as they are.

Power likes
"the Truth."

It uses it
to kill you.

IV.

Hermes resists.
Neither evil

nor righteous,
Hermes, the dark child,

will not be denied
his right to be more

than a smart
inconvenience.

He gets what he wants,
casts moonlight nets

over rote and possession.
He's refused

to be abandoned,
does whatever it takes.

Even in the faceless
mass of the dead

we have our faces
in his eyes.

Hermes knows
how to flow,

he asks no deforming compromise.
Our shadows are his friends.

He doesn't mind
the dark side of our minds.

He knows what it means
to be unpreferred,

to live on the edge
of light and shade,

to be invisible
and suspected,

to be beyond the limits
of love and trust,

beyond the limits of the tamed.
Hermes trusts the bumbling,

the fragile, the shaded,
the twitch of truth,

takes comfort in
the genuine fool

who loses his way
through the easiest day

distracted by stars
he cannot forget.

Hermes takes the other side.
Nothing is too good for him,

too dark for him,
too absurd, too mean,

too alone,
too disastrous, chaotic,

unredeemed.
When you lose

what you cannot do without,
when you lose

what you know cannot be lost,
take Hermes by the hand

and be a child
along for the ride.

He will take you back
to where you started,

changed
and the same. ■

Aphrodite

I.

Aphro-
dite.

Put your tongue
and mind

around
and in

that holy name
and see how sex

undresses
revelation.

Beneath the folds,
the melodies of stone,

Her truth
is regular as rhythm,

regular as scent,
as leaves in sun

feeding with abandon,
as birds

without reason
flocking

regular as petals,
intractable,

uncatchable
as roots.

In the garden,
Aphrodite mates

wild flower fields
with rose promenades,

the feral
with the seeded

the unplanned, expected,
with the unforeseen.

Curved,
soft, tight,

sex for Her
is serious

as the body
that she loves,

serious
as a melody of order

in the wilderness
of kindness

where beauty "strikes,
confounds, and overwhelms."

Here "everything
is sacred,

even
the profane,"

She said, stroking
his shoulder.

"The sacred
is.

Nothing else
may be,"

She sighed,
as the fog was drawn around them.

Goddess of mercy,
of sea swells,

hip flows, ribbons
draped on waists,

you are
the truest fate,

the only sympathy
the cosmos gives

in the beauty
of its burning.

II.

Shockingly,
blamelessly,

we fall in love
with bodies, minds,

with souls
and lives,

their differences undone
by Aphrodite's smile.

She knows
no difference.

She knows
where the body

of the universe
might be touched,

its delectable
groves

of thought
and skin.

She shows us how
lovers have no room

for Hiroshima,
ethnic cleansing.

There's no room at all
for parents to commit atrocities

once or twice
before supper.

With no difference,
we can love

what we desire,
every cloud,

every shoulder,
every sunny spot,

every piece of shade.
And all things seem

so right
that we desire tenderness

with what we've made
and can never make,

with trees and wind,
with coves and deserts,

cemeteries, books,
hawks and cities,

the scarred
and the flawless—

all as beautiful
as our lovers are

with
or without us.

III.

"Now
is first.

Now
is all,"

She told him,
smoothing his brow,

he smiled, smoothing
his palm on Her knee.

"Love
now

as you
love yourself,"

She smiled.
Some gods of love

would kill you
to save you.

Aphrodite
doesn't save you,

doesn't kill you;
she turns her back on you

if you deny her even once.
When Aphrodite sings

the hymn of the nerves,
there is no denial

without death.
If she can't loosen your grip

then you're already
buried alive.

But never
confuse

Her love
with pleasure.

Pleasure has
its ethics:

never cause
much pain.

Pleasure is
the mask of love, not

its mysterious,
far smile.

Never confuse
pain with love;

love is free,
love is free

of all defilement;
what is not free

is not
love.

IV.

Pygmalion fell in love
with the image of Love,

with her statue
in fact,

as Narcissus fell
for himself.

I fell
in awe

at twenty-one,
fell

for philosophy,
the first time

I saw
the Venus of Cyrene,

and, so transformed,
I could understand

how desire
is holy,

is life's
pure dream

of the best
for itself,

that the flooding
I'd felt

from childhood was not
the sin

of the wickedness
of nerves.

The falling,
the swelling,

the tending,
the stroking,

the kissing,
the joying—

as a boy, they were all
lost on me

in my need to escape
through the skin, until

that moment
when I saw Her

in the very stone,
nude as a galaxy,

pure as the code
in my genes.

V.

Truth releasing
Aphrodite,

candor
smoother,

intimate
kneader,

smile lover,
calm giver:

When the body
of the cosmos

—its Spring
and its thoughts—

when the body
of the cosmos

is what we love,
then everything

is sacred.
To be in love

with time,
with chance,

like Sappho
loved her students,

perfumed
in desire's garden,

to love God that way,
the Mind, the Tao,

to love that way
heals the cosmos,

one life at a time,
of the line we've drawn

in the dust of our minds
—although, in loving all

we must in turn
love both

the line
and both

sides of the line.
Once it is,

it is
to be loved

in Aphrodite's
inexhaustible mercy

which is Her joy,
our Odyssey

fulfilled by Her
before we start.

For all love
feels to her

like a memory
of perfection.

That's how we know
to trust

the completion
that has no end. ■

Athena

Wisdom is an armed rebellion,
a pure uprising to restrain

and break apart the rules,
scorn the use of ice maps in the desert,

overthrow the impulse
to dead habit.

In the dirty wars, the random voids, the moral tics
of Wallstreet, Gulags, Los Alamos, or any place like Argentina,

Athena in Her wisdom
dispossesses the absurd;

so flexible She is unexpectable;
She catches the rigid and the stupid,

the tyrant-thieves off guard. In secret,
She advises us, Odysseus and the rest,

to be
if not

right,
not wrong,

to be unfathomable and like
an unstoppable knife,

like Her:
silent as eyes.

Athena, warring with the obvious,
understands unboundedness.

Owl smooth,
night victor,

"tameless," knowing how to do
what She wants every time,

She is so patient, She wins
with no loss of love.

Wisdom is
generosity.

Athena wants
Odysseus to do

who he knows he should be.
She gives him certainty

in disguise
as friendship he can trust

to never blind him,
never punish him

for truth.
She sees to him,

sees to it
that he can't be compromised

while his will to strive, Her first
defining gift to him, still thrives.

So both are chaste, in their own ways.
Odysseus chaste of immortality,

so mortal his purity appeals
to Wisdom's love of everything.

Athena, pure of all negation:
She even makes Penelope's sly chastity so wise

her patience seems to her like sleep.
To earn the prize of prizes,

Athena's loving gaze, which, gray-eyed, knows
all differences of shade,

we must be, first, like Her
without Her help,

unforgiving, without fatigue,
inventing as easily as breathing,

as much at peace with yes and no
as maybe not and maybe so.

Peace conserves. Anger, She abhors it,
the infrugality of war.

But once She's crossed, She never loses.
Imagine! Never loses. Her rule:

never trust the rules,
never think you know enough;

trust chance, jujitsu dance with it,
erase defeat, open your brain and let it go,

rely on no one
until you'd bet your life on her,

give,
give,

give,
give,

look to wisdom, as She smiles on you,
with a giving, grateful smile.

Athena has no wiles;
crafty with conscience,

she outsmarts everyone at knowing
who Her friends really are.

Say to her, my brain is open,
please move in.

She knows the ropes, which strands of contradiction
strangle us, which true ambivalence is safe to show.

She is our true transparency.
With Her we can always

see through our selves.
She's why we keep on course,

why we sense there is a course at all,
a way that is ours, given to us as it happens,

an integrity through time
that we can never see,

without Her ease,
the example of Her endless view,

so like the ease of having been
when you know

how it's all worked out
before it has. ■

Poseidon

Infinitely unburdened
as You are, Poseidon,

by moral sublimations,
You are not

immoral, nor
moral-less

like more or less the rest of timelessness.
You are just

immune
to decision, serene

as skin can be in memory
safe from pain, moving always

where You can
with the force

of the un-
drainable.

Nothing can keep you
forever

from filling who, or where, You will.
You make

all ways
Your own,

seeping, carving,
infusing, exploding.

Few have seen Your unboundedness
break through

our desperation
to stop You up.

I just know seaside, sand,
Your waves

that come like breaths so regular
even their deep

inhalations
are expected.

Earth shaker,
engulfer,

liquid of Love's
emergence from the foam,

God of the sea in the womb,
amniotic force and calm,

You are the first
settler, filler of voids,

follower of the least resistance.
You go where You are

unimpeded,
like all

respectful lovers go,
god of the simplest flow.

I know You as the only place
of all the places that I know

that feels to me
like I feel when I'm free

to feel exactly who I am
beyond what fate demands

with its distractions.
Moving

is what matters first;
it's Your law.

That's why you've never brushed me off.
I mustn't stop.

I ran to You once in baby glee.
You did not drink me under.

So now I trust You with my parents' dust.
You've become

imagination's
space,

the place it goes to forget
the facts.

Even the first
rapture of the mind I knew,

my first
nonsexual lust,

came from You in a sunny gale
when I was seventeen

on the deck of an old Dutch wreck
hearing *La Mer* with my eyes

in a glass-box music room,
so close to brine,

the music stank of salt and blood,
the perfume of true love.

God of all waters,
Great Father of menace and marvel,

of the promise that flows in my ditch,
the sea swell in my tomatoes,

just hearing you breathe,
just Your smell,

Your rank life, in Maine,
Your fog in Malibu, lifts me

beyond my weight,
like at Schoodic Point

when I watched you
polishing the continent,

caressing through
distraction as the moon

moved through You
with her rocking

and the bottomless
weight of her heart.

Father of Cyclops, Pegasus,
lover of Medusa, Odysseus's plague,

Lord of anomalies,
always local, odd, dependable,

supremely
world bound, free as stars

washing onto gravity's
invincible,

receding shore,
no amount of diapers,

deck chairs, unprocessed shit,
nor all contagion's needles, latex gloves,

pull tabs, packaging,
Styrofoam and crude,

nor all the shoes, the cans,
the orange rinds and evidence,

nothing will break You
of Your irresistible   ·

disdain
for the comedy we dump

all over You
to claim You

ours, another
colony of folly.

We are *yours*.
You are what we are,

dangerous, immense, horrible, sublime,
but so

intimate, so
unsettling and frail, You will

evaporate with us
when the sun

death-grins at us
in its last

gasp flame out,
boiling everything

to erase
all hope

in memory's space, that thin
veil of recollection, undulating now

like a cool white sheet
on sea-breeze evenings

just before a child
forgets she's not asleep. ■

Artemis

Bear mother, supple,
child-tumbling, ferocious,

hair-raising
with love,

Great Artemis, cyclone
of perfection,

She is called Kallisto,
the most beautiful

in Her playing
and in Her rage.

Goddess of unmarred snow,
of nine-year-old girls,

of magma, infancy,
of inner poise, integrity,

all boundlessness,
the holy spirit of the undisturbed,

we hear of Her still
on a mesa of grasses,

and sage steppes,
ungrazed Artemisia

moon gray,
untouched for ten thousand years,

in Utah,
not Arkadia,

the goddess of No Man's Mesa
who won't tolerate

being looked at,
and is never to be touched.

Scar roads through Her meadows
and she knows no mercy.

She is everywhere
we've never been,

the goddess of places no one should go.
In the moonlight of forever,

we can barely see
menageries of spring born

dancing in Her honor
in the perfect

place before beginning
which never ends.

That's as close to Her
as we may get:

observers of strange dancing.
We must praise Her

far way
in our minds.

Great Artemis, savior
of the unexplored,

goddess of the feral
who loathes extinctions,

who is the cause of all extinction,
mistress of the fittest

and the least fit,
of all that is fruitful

in itself, for no
other purpose,

Goddess, when nothing clean and early
is left upon the earth,

when what we *do*
with consciousness

leaves our minds
so muscle-bound

we're paralyzed
confusing power

with survival,
will You stop us,

take the world back from us,
year by disastrous year?

Or will you save
what's left of us that's wild,

teach us,
how to free ourselves again,

how to be
untamed, like You,

by appetite and grasping,
by the yokes

of status and possession,
luxury and speed?

You are never
not free, even now.

And we are waiting.
We know You will make something happen,

some terrible change
we could never foretell

—like leaves turning poison,
or birds farting smog,

like skin
eating muscle,

or dirt
eating seeds

—something will shake us,
will force us

to submit,
collapse,

renew.
And from the debris,

the die off,
the judgment

of cause and effect,
You will arise

clean as all beginnings
in minds

craving freedom
more than license,

liberty more
than plenty. ■

Demeter

Humor is
the god of peace,
as your smile,
divine
with the bounty of grief,
is steel
for miraculous will,
prying free
the heart child
to walk
resolute with Spring,
out of the fortress of greed,
the smothering shroud of profit,
death's sterile garden
of force and bone.
There is no love
in rape, in seduced demand,
no love at all
in "it's just business."

What you cannot be
who you are without,
you find a way
to free. ■

Hestia

Nothing lives without You.
Nothing can exist

without its gravity,
its density, integrity,

its central calm
ordering without containing,

containing
without stifling,

allowing the maximum
disorder

without decay,
so even

randomness flows
with the regularity of stars.

Only Hestia,
in perfect

pointedness,
can never waver,

never tip,
never flutter or expire;

only She remains
while always moving on

—for She is the opening
and the flooding,

the banks and the tide,
the root and what is rooted,

meaning and shape at the same time.
First, eternal,

before and after,
She is our trust

in being tomorrow,
the abstract

and the fact.
Hestia, so calm,

the motion of rock
through a ripple,

She is the vanishing change,
the center and its wake.

All hope and all decay
move out from Her,

come back to Her,
Great Source,

Great Home,
Great Eye

drinking sight
to the depths of light. ■

Chaos

    The space-flinging, time-singing
    unborn
Goddess First-Of-All,
Chaos The Free:
    She casts the stars,
      the comets, moons, the dust of light,
casts the flocks and flowers, any way they go.
She needs
    no control.
    She strolls,
cloud flowing,
at her own pace,
    fearless as motion,
    being what happens
just as it does.
She's so unlike us
    utterly
    in Her essence,
so unlike us
She can stand
    the freedom
    of everything else,
stand it
and give it,
    and praise it
    as it follows itself
always
back to Her.

That's the migration
we can't resist:
Our best is Hers
when we become
      so unlike ourselves,
      so free,
that we can stand
not to know
      where we're going,
      can stand
not to make safe
the freedom
      of those we love,
      always ripening in ourselves
the peace that is
where it is going. ■

Ares

Snake brain, slaughterer,
it's you who thought to make

napalm stick under water,
you who flew the nightmare planes

into the nightmare buildings, who budgeted
plastic land mines for blowing off feet.

It's you, not Strangelove the inventor.
Bodies are troughs for you.

So why are you loved by The Lover?
Are giants all cuddly

when caught on their La-Z-Boy sofas
their teeth in a cup,

wearing their scuff-about slippers?
What's with it,

this loving of dangerous men?
Does She just adore Your

reflex, true abandon?
It's hypocrisy to blame you.

Each of us might need you
if the brutal bastard's gone berserk

and all we can do
is go for his eyeballs

and balls, and fight to the end
with no end but his.

Mostly, though, we need to keep culture on,
zipped up, Athena combing our hair

and telling us exactly
how to cream you, bowl You over

with elegant force,
You for whom

charred wounds
are a pheromone.

The Spartans knew.
No hecatombs of oxen for you;

only a human barbecue would do.
Everyone hates you

until they need you.
Then they pray when you're through

they won't hear your teeth on their bones.
You're all about

nothing
in between.

That's why
we may win

with your gorging,
but your shit won't come out of our souls.

We stink with you, shamed,
suicidal,

worth
less.

You're useless
for all tasks but one:

Torn shreds
and pieces of us—indecipherable

gore—
that's all you've ever done. ■

Hephaestus

Lord of the "technical
sweetness of it all,"*

your genius can pound
tanks out of stone,

steady the proud
wild life of clocks,

play fountain pens
rivering poems from golden nibs.

You're as much a god of Tiffany
Easter egg elites, as the patron saint

of farriers and stevedores,
of Eric Hoffer minding the store

while he does his best thinking
on company time.

Loner divine, disobedient, sure minded
you hide yourself behind

the dazzle-masks of what you make,
all of you except

———————————————————

*Quote from J. Robert Oppenheimer.

the welding-spark geysers of your hair,
and your golden, cat half eyes

unbearable as magma.
Every time I jerryrig a garden hose,

or fix a hoe, or twist
a paper clip to keep my glasses on

I think of You with your lunch pail and thermos,
belching fumes,

forgetting you're alone,
hunched over,

tinkering in your old garage.
They say you can cure

snakebite and madness. I'm sure
there's nothing you can't fix

except Your own love life.
Those golden nets look great

on Aphrodite's hips,
but she slips right through them,

like stepping from a slippery shift
shimmering at her ankles.

Why wouldn't there be a sorrowing to you,
a posture that hints of sick dejection,

like sweat stains are
telltale signs

on the coolest beauty
stepping into lunch.

It's touch you want.
I've touched the hulls you've made,

the metal skins of ships and planes,
and thought of you stroking

the smoothness of their seams
like one might brush the inside of a thigh

with the passing, tender graze of a wrist.
Huge, strong as a man who must

walk on his arms, we see your soul
roaring out of silos, landing on the moon with us;

you gave Mr. Gatling
the genius of impatience for his gun;

such a range: The god of gadgets,
computers, nano processors and bayonets,

false teeth, cyclotrons, cotton gins, and toasters.
Your golden braces hide

the strength to make the light bulb glow,
to turn the dam's roar into cinema

and love notes on the Internet;
You don't invent the problems;

they come to you to find
solutions to exist.

The deep injustice of the crimes
come all the time, come all the time.

Summer time and the killing is easy;
the dead are never repaired

even with your mapless,
inexhaustible head.

We praise our days
that You, the fates,

the dunce hearts
who rule the thrilling world

can never kill us
more than once. ■

Asclepias

Perfect
comforter, clean
doctor
calling our dreams
to heal us,
our unchained
trust
to end our pain,
immortality
was your one
transgression:
Not your own vice,
but the sin
of arrogance
in the service
of compassion:

Zeus
crushed you
for it.

Death,
the only escape,
—to deny it
out of virtue
is to invite
misfirings,
slipups, mishandlings
that even the Gods can't
untangle.
Death is their treasure for us,
their sure and simple
sublime-minded cure. ■

Zeus

Zeus, you're last. I thought
I liked you least.
I mean no disrespect.

It's just your alpha
cock, invincible jock-
strap bully-self

angered me like a cat
angers a mouse
uselessly.

Past sixty, a sweaty gray beard too,
I see I have confused you
with what kings and kids

do to gods. You're not
to me anymore a dumbbell
Hitler clown, a Ronald

McDonald Pol Pot
with blitz bolts blazing
a morbid, sizzling

narcissistic conviction that you,
just you alone, have the right
to be right.

You're no superego,
amoral censor hypocrite
neatener of feeling either. Are you?

How could you be?
You may look like a joke
pathology;

but you are the god
father, the sire
perdu, missing in action

alone at the top,
a man's man no man
can emulate, so

masculine, so
king of the hill, so
like Hef the Colossus,

only little skip-roping girls
can play hide and seek with you
without incurring the divine

ambiguity of your
celestial genetics.
No power but

humor's logic
could crack you up.
You're not smothered

by women; you're smothered
in women;
they enthuse you, let you use

your climatic
aphrodisiac,
giddy with your

preposterous big
fun to be king thing.
Mortal men must never

do as you do.
You don't like that. Right?
You make them pay

the ultimate price
for amusing you
without delighting you.

So some of them
remade you to look
like themselves—silent,

threatening,
unpredictable, aloof,
scared

brain hollow
by women's power,
happy nowhere except

with rude maidens
in the dark woods
and bowers of their dreams.

And yet, god father
it is You, The Listener,
supplicants pray to.

You are the one
who hears and gives
the answers we need

through the voice
in our heads. Desperate,
without knowing

why, I asked long ago,
"What am I to do now?"
And you told me

like a Roshi lumberjack:
"Pay attention. Be calm.
Get out of the way.

Polish the mountain.
You are your experience
of the divine."

It was you
who answered me,
ancient voice

before text upon text.
I asked,
and I received.

It still happens. I
evoke the spirit
of Apollo and apologize

to You. Your name
is another name,
with others and others,

for trustworthy power.
If the universe can
be trusted, it's because

you're a non-
sanctimonious wiseacre, sage
joker of out of the blue

lightning conundrums
and shocking
suspicions of sense.

A god of passion?
Of course you are.
A god of wild desire? Of course.

A god women like?
Well, sure
if it wasn't for Her.

Women who know their freedom
is divine
are stronger than you,

greater than doubt and reason,
greater than sense and restraint.
And men?

We're still stupid enough
to risk thunder:
to run around in Zeus suits

and big bolts
of blazing. But You hate
copycats;

You flatten us out just
at the moment of our first
prime achievements, each one of us

humbled to a char
by the size
of our pleasure's lost causes. ■

Hera

Hera, You're last,
not Zeus, I thought; I feared You most,
Great Queen of the marriage torture farce,

deep keeper of the chains, the guilt press
and the script of blame.
Are You the monster mommy passive guilt magician

Homer scorned with witless panic, a dust-bunny boy dread,
under the bed, depressed into a cosmic horror?
What are You?

I feel about You like a hiker feels about a grizzly
rising from the bushes
ten feet away,

like my sense of justice feels
for Clytemnestra
who got royally shafted,

and shafted back, and then got
abandoned in the back
because she dared to push

the obvious beyond
quaint jailhouse chores and the chastity
gag of wifehood.

Are You so despised,
and horror-
tease even

the ultimate
naughty stud god
Casanova Zeus Priapus,

just because you're a woman
doing a man's work
in a man's trap, a cave

of recrimination,
vendetta's moll
harder than any

anvil brain
cocksure
of its righteous, numb

know-nothing power?
You're not just Homer's
ogre-in-law, are you,

the arch mommy drudge
burping the Big Guy guzzler
of everyone's

clout? You're at least
the force of gulled expectation,
aren't You, the dark strength

of the bilked, of those who depend
on promises no one ever
has the secrecy to keep?

I don't know.
Could you ever have guessed you'd become
the vile

mistress of the norm, the bitter
possessor, conformity's
Inquisitor, model of models

of how it should be
in horrors of convention?
You did blind a prophet,

made blessed intoxication
go cannibal mad,
brutalized innocence seduced

for being innocent,
tortured bastards
and made lovers

into sexless trees,
and fly-tortured,
milk-swollen cows.

Maybe You're
the goddess still
most friendly

to all who believe
they know
the whole bargain

then are brought to their knees,
forced to agree
they'll have to make do

with The Mystery
as all they can count on
after all.

Fidelity to You is like that, isn't it?
A disaster beyond
the moral, gross

inferiority of that
lightning prick
with whom you have

no choice
but to make do.
It's not just

that you're a stickler
for the rules,
for any rules, is it?

Should Zeus
have confided in you,
told the whole truth?

Withholding—
was that His crime?
Would you have seen

confession
as fidelity
or just a trap

set by a fool
for himself?
I'll say this.

No one can regret
true being
and what it forces us

to express.
Is that Your law—
only for You?

What are You?
You're not
the eternal feminine,

any more than He's
the Olympian, brassknuckled
Bumstead. Sex is

more than the grinder
of razor illusions,
more than the mighty, damned

do-as-I-please
big bruiser.
I see you both

as junk shop
salt and pepper shakers
with all

the infinite
other
condiments, delectables and chances

revealed to us
in very
tiny,

faint type
on the empty back
end of the menu. ■

Heracles

We praise you,
amazed and ashamed
we look so alike,
our butcher's aprons
pink with death . . .
if only we could perform
our routine
impossibilities with such
redundant genius,
but for us to claim
virtue victorious,
and not succumb
to madness and slaughter,
effort
requires of us
tasks like dust,
so many
they make us prey
to prodigal
impatience
as vulnerable
as your muscle,
which is, after all,
in a different condition,
just
meat to be sliced
like biceps
resemble an apple
to a butcher knife. ■

Orpheus

You are the source
of all of us who work like this.
We know you by heart.

We can't help it.
You humble us,
each of us, sweet and low, even

the critically deluded,
the Hannibal poets
and their elephant egos, even

the gatekeepers
doling out prizes to clones,
the academic concierges

with treasure maps
to the ancient shrine of the whores
and the dens

of other guilds they feign
on a first name basis.
You play on all of us.

I remember the first time I saw
her shadow blue veins, the lace
of the Nile near her neck

on the fan of her brown, undersoft,
shore smooth chest,
that pulse I saw

above the top button.
When I think like this,
are you remembering too?

Was it a sight like that
that made You the Master
Genius of Loneliness?

Is this what happens
when we think like You,
when we feel what You let us feel

of what's inside You?
How can we thank You, then,
for these sweet chains

that free us of all
our numb impossibilities?
We know You can make depression dance

like the rocks dance when they're not themselves.
I know You are the proof
of all that's unaccountable,

of mountains of air
in spiraling columns circling
moon paths in rings of wind

orbiting the mind, which has
no gravity to contain it.
What do I know of You,

except what I say
when I'm more than myself?
Can I say, then, that You're

the god of And,
of over and over,
of on-going, of no

opposite, no apart,
of everything that has
no heat, no weight, the god of all

that can't be measured except through the world
you alter and affect?
How can I not

know who You are
when You give me
plum blossoms geysering

white through noon light,
the sun so endlessly swaying.
How can I not? I know

how death disgusts You.
I couldn't stomach it either, married
body and soul for the first time,

when it threatened to block
the flowering of her breath
just as we'd forgotten

how to be so alone.
And what of your wyrd?
Your singing head,

your dismemberment,
your double grief?
Must you always look back

against the deal
to have it all?
Of course you must.

You live forever in And,
never in Either Or.
You had her back.

The blood rivers fanned behind your eyes,
her blue lace flooded with spring.
You wanted to have her

and know you had,
and you had that too.
And you lost her again.

And
is not all
addition.

Is that
what her deaths
are fated to mean? ■

Hades

Us in our unbelievable billions . . .
You take all of us on, of course,
the young, the ripe, the sublime, the old

dictator shot by his own cheap assassins,
the poets, sweethearts, empowering teachers,
young mothers, the dead

poor, the dead rich, even the tortured
who think they'll never die;
You take us all, and yet

You're not much Yourself; You're not
a composite of us at all. If You're not
everyone we've ever been,

I can't say You're exactly a grave
or a stomach either. Your essence is
a meaty zero. Your myths

are all but nonexistent, like You,
an almost blank, except for that
abduction and the final deal,

sending love back and forth
in Persephone's skin
like a child of divorce

out of death's bleak, equal
compassion; and we mustn't forget
Your supporting role

as a monster of the sentimental
whose native state
is the kingdom of grief.

It's that myth of You being swayed
like plague fever is swayed
by a cold cloth on the brow for a while,

swayed by the more
beautiful grief of art,
caught between fact and time, refusing

everything it can to You.
What a god of death You are!
Orpheus unglued you. You The Never Known,

your strict nonbeing swayed by a song.
But then, there's that cold shadow of You
as the dirty tricker who never lets go,

whose duty must always prevail,
who can make anyone look over their shoulder
just by telling them not to.

I think I know this much about You:
You are the God of Neither
and the God of Nor. And we don't like it.

Our stories of You have odd visiting hours
and travelers who come and go
looking to know the future

as if the mine of the past could tell them
what the present can't.
But we know up here, deep in our rank DNA,

that no one ever comes back from You.
When Orpheus sang the dog to sleep
crossed the threshold alive and came to court,

he amused You, You another lonely man stunned
by the weakness of his needs,
whose rule is a mad taste of loss.

For him, You were a dream
and dying, a Morpheus ode;
for You, Your own nature is just

the bare, true sadness of arithmetic:
of one and no other, of one
and no two, of one

and then none.
Nothing adds up
but zero.

God of Once, God of Next,
we come to you in our countlessness each day
like virga

vanishing, or, horribly,
still substantial and bewildered,
waiting for our nexts.

Lord of Nothing,
Lord of Never, None, and Nil, Lord Hades,
an emptiness that's always filled,

You evade definition,
our hysteric naming,
and if we try too hard,

You trick us with our own
brain's relentless stain:
our crass,

matter-of-fact
refusal
to suspend

disbelief in a fair,
barely
inscrutable Mind

that finds
definition to be
a ratty, cheap

interruption, a rash
on your sweet,
inconsolable sleep. ■

Dionysus

Player, hider, healer,
god of fun, of masks and scars,

of giddy hope and idiocy
sublime,

of cruelty's will
rending minds

blurred always
in lost forgetting,

always rendered in return
by disbelief's remembering,

Dionysus, dear,
you're all at once

this trapping jumble:
savage, jolly,

hopeless, lost,
lord of places that create us

like costumes, makeup
recreate us. Energy of all

transformation, guardian of
unconscious chances,

denying You feels
like trying to become You:

it jams our brains
so nothing works,

a sticky mess
of technicolor stars

that leads to grim
absurdities of death

by abstinence erupting
or indulgence

imploding on the floor.
We must find how to find You

in the long calm of ourselves
where You have chosen us

and chosen for us
the proscenium

of the muses
rising

from the neural sea.
Make-believe doesn't need

falling down drunk-
dreaming magicians, though a few can't hurt.

That's not who You are.
Even in Euphoria we can

feel Your
obligation

to proportion
from time to time.

It's all of You that matters.
Without the whole,

the wobbles are quite fatal.
Your double birth, in fact,

balances and unlocks
the box within a box

of You, the hidden all
of what You give us,

those parts of You
that invent

appearance, invent
seeming,

embody
beloved illusion,

permitting us to be
the likeness of another,

or even the likeness
of who we want to be

but are not yet.
The play's the thing.

Readiness is all.
It's not just masks

of make-believe You give us,
it's masks of promise,

roles that form us,
jobs that build us,

parts to play that
make us act in ways

beyond us
when we play ourselves.

And what does this
alchemy

of becoming who we seem to be
have to do with

loosening,
with the vast, mysterious

nether facts
of image

and imagination
as world altering weathers?

Is the liquid genius
of the vine

nature's code,
its Open Sesame

to states of mind that trick us
even with ourselves?

Apollo has the map
but You are pure

potentiality.
Without You

nothing would change,
order would prevail;

no humor, aberration,
no wisdom

from experience would undermine
the burdens of our long

rehearsed and boring dooms.
Revolution would remain

a seed suspended
in the death fraud of perfection.

Dionysus, You surprise
even puppets

so they speak their secret minds.
You give us

a way to be mad
that is usefully

sane seeming,
even, at times,

harmlessly
sound and obscure.

Your masks,
filtering

the purity
of truth without

self-consciousness,
unbridle us with health.

And when we dream
You pour Yourself

right through us
in mysteries

of meaning
distant as

pure knowing is
in minds that cannot tell

dreams from art,
art from fact,

truth from what
is always real:

that players are
who they pretend to be;

that stories are
a force

as powerful as storms;
that what we tell ourselves

can kill us or transform us
into health. It is You

who can unleash scenarios of war
and aphrodisiacs in solstice dreams.

We must believe You.
The penalties of rote

and ugly reason
for stupidities

of disbelief,
and going only

by the numbers,
force us to fall

so free,
so deep for You

we never doubt
your trickster griefs

and foolish joys that apprehend
more than blank wisdom ever comprehends. ■

Apollo

God of Rules, of vatic
trance and minds

agile as the dolphin's dance,
god of freedom's

patterns,
the charities

of restraint
like sonnets are

the formal wherewithal
to be a certain way:

God of channels, power surges,
Hermes's champion, dupe,

and bartered brother,
your goodness comes to us, Apollo,

when with apologies we're filled
with effortless rejoining

as ego's noose
falls loose like Christmas ribbon.

Apollo, so beautiful you are,
so full of shine

and light that moves
faster than itself,

so fast it arrives
before it's left,

like the question put
into the asker's head

so Zeus can answer it
before she voices it.

God of the fateful right and wrong,
as in the odd right ways to make a song

and the infinite wrong ways
it dribbles

formless, dull, excreted
even when you play it

just perfect right
—the pure bones

of your temple
in Arcadia, its formal

nakedness of stone
shorn of accident

in the wild, full emptiness
of nature's body,

it is like who we are,
and so are You;

relationships
define us.

It's like that, too, with girls,
god of the perfect tune,

you're either in tune
or you're striking out.

What is it with You
that makes them flee,

agree to love You
then deny You?

What is it in your godhead
that repels them? The perfection

of your youth
and its supreme

hardheadedness
horrific in its innocent

all wanting? Zeus,
the old smoothie, knew

what to do with his.
Even your successes

don't go right, like Cyrene,
the perfect Venus form

who bore you
the beekeeper dunce

who Eurydice, the bride,
died trying to escape;

even the glory of Cyrene
caused tragedies of love

cascading in your wake.
Everything has a rightness

that rules right through it.
Even abandon has.

Dionysus knew it.
You invented rules

to be broken by him.
You broke them too,

like a ruler
with a straying edge.

At Your best,
You're true, the power

of the guiding no
that lets the guiding yes flood in;

the power of the shaping limit,
of truth beyond perception

that allows perception;
the power of the grounded real,

the ideal that has no form until
a madness makes it so.

When reason is
devious with power,

love's deep sense
is infected first.

You were never meant to be
a statuesque, golden boy,

Galahad, dragon slaying
teen with abs of stone.

You are the truth
without us,

I once said, the truth
which is without us

"only pure."
You are young!

So young, yet always
gorgeous wise, voluptuous

as reason's tricks
breaking through

your oracle, Zeus's playfulness
riddling through her

like your music
plays Bach's heart,

your fugue tamer,
corralling even

unbreakable Pan.
God of perfect

patterns
and such passion

even time forgets itself with You,
we all love You

as we love our youth,
as we love the perfect, lucid,

tragedy, the longed-for truth
of being young without exception,

perfectly
contradictory, perfect

in our beauty's pain,
rarer, in our minds,

than all things rare.
Who is it at the pool

smiling at his smile?
Who can hold a mirror

to rationality's coy youth?
Who can calculate the damage

of reason's adolescent years?
Who can keep the flayer's knife

so sharp it melts
through living hide

like a tantrum's razor wish?
Who's the healer, arrow sprayer,

plague infester, hot head,
Phoebus, constantly reborn?

Who can build the perfect
bombs and rockets

while always glad to show the girls
what's really in his pocket?

Who combines the darkest
and the fairest, the brightest

good, the cruelest
absolute, irrational perfection?

You hit the mark Apollo.
If something's in the way

you tame it, cure it,
or shoot right through it. ■

Pan

Startling as cats laughing, as mastiffs
whistling a happy tune, Pan is Great,

the fast god of fear,
of "get the hell outta here" grizzly fear,

of adrenaline blasts,
squirrels darting from eagles,

kids squealing in panicked joy
at a wiggly odd ugly old bug. Brainy,

feral, Pan is
as we are: both

earth born
and more,

as the world without us is
still holy.

On his haunches, tail switching,
horns laid back, adored,

He casts his dice with Aphrodite, teaching Her
the chances, taught by Her that skin

is god-awful holy too.
And Pan, with his fabulous,

indifferent
strangeness,

the force of all
that's not supposed to be,

Aphrodite knows
that Pan is great

because he is like her:
sublime beyond validity,

prooflessly real.
And when the temples were closed down, sealed false

by piety in AD 391, when even the sun
was stripped of its holy place, multiplicity

deposed, the curtains on Olympus closed,
the sets dismantled, the scripts and part books

folded in a trunk,
Great Pan is dead, they said.

But He isn't,
never will be. He kept the dice,

fended off the suffering god
who absorbed from the earth

its ceaseless resurrection.
Pan remains

like us,
eternally born,

and earns
our jumpy, hot respect

each day we choose
the mischievous truth

of ourselves,
refusing to be tamed.

Monster dear, darling beast
we think we're not,

God of our indispensable mental defeats,
when panic saves us

from thinking ourselves
onto the platter of death,

You are Great, nymph dancer,
blessed with deep noontime snoozes

that perfume out to us
even now

to drug us with surprised affection.
You are here in our longing,

in our wisest fears
of immobility

and crushing rule,
always here, blossoming up through freeways,

sidewalks, concrete curbs, the weed
no order can keep out.

Dear Pan,
master of grace

in the Holy Mess we thrive in,
teach us how

to learn to be loved
again and again,

like beasts who finally
trust enough, and keep on trusting,

so truth and play
may dance

the serious depths together,
safe, calm, wild, fast, and unafraid. ∎

from *Hymns to Aphrodite*

For Sappho

I.

Love can't be told
what to do,
who to love,
who to leave,
who to scare
out of his wits.
Love can't be told
anything,
any more than a rock in space can be told
to miss the gardener
kissing his lover on the lawn.

II.

The skin
on your back,
the heat
in your spine,
tastes
like your thoughts
praised
in my mouth.

III.

He loved
to kiss with her.
It was simple.
There was
no why,
no serious
because.
He loved
to feel her skin
with the eyes
of his hands.
For him
kissing her
and touching her
were no different
from waking up
—simple,
holy,
glorious,
with no answer,
no question,
no doubt.

IV.

Sex can't
help itself.
You jump from a tree,
you fall;
you spray yourself with a hose,
you get wet;
you feel a wanting
and you want.
This helplessness
has little to do
with locking doors
and bodies
bathing in each other
like light through waves.
Sex is the mad
thrilling before
the first touching.
The rest
is something else,
is like play
but seismic,
underground
truths
shifting
and trembling, and thus
so seriously
fun.

VII.

A working man and his little boy
practice casting for fish in the heat,
exquisitely
flicking out
hope
onto the dust
of a vacant lot
beneath a snarling overpass
—such rapture,
their lines
of desire
rippling through the dusk
like us
practicing each other
over and over
until we know
nothing's better
than getting it right.

VIII.

Some distances
can be forgotten
in bed,
some even
disappear
like streams lost in sand,
but keeping

the distance to breathe
on our own
so there is
some distance
to forget in bed,
that's the secret
we have made our own.

IX.

I'm alone.
You're everywhere
but where I am
exactly.
I'm jumpy.
The music tastes bad.
I want you
to close in on me,
unzip thought
from skin.
I want to feel
cool light
flow from your heat,
my whole
body and soul
resting more
in touching you
than it does
from paradisal
sleep.

X.

Smoke
from forest fires
feels like this,
wild with scent,
blinding, white,
choking out,
drowning us
down and out,
dark
as closing our eyes.
Only a hollow
will help,
a space to hide in,
to breathe on our own,
and then
back to the fire
and searing fog.

XI.

Taking care
of your skin,
taking the most
delicate care
of your brain cape,

your nerve shore
as it folds
inside you,

taking care of your muscles,
your knots,
the energy fists
that can't
unclinch without my fingers,
taking care of you like this
is the same as seeing
the soft
round sides
of the moon
caress across
the small
of Aphrodite's
back so warm
chills vanish
with her passing.

XII.

Everything I can think of right now
has something to do with how
ageless you look to me
in my glee
at seeing you again
with five minutes gone,
again and again
and over again,
each time my delight
at your face
simply takes up all the room
my mind has for time.

XV.

Of course
the old fall in love
or stay that way
in ways
that would weaken
the weaker.
Age only means
years and years
of youth's single advantage:
not knowing you're not
meant to risk
every
predictable ease
just to go on
feeling exactly like this.

XVI.

The truth is
Love is
you and me.
Aphrodite
comes
to shore
on the foam
of the willing
between us.
Love is not

without us,
or without
them over there
in their billions.
She's a forest
so tangled
in slow dancing,
the branching
of birth,
new life
splurging out
through life as it is,
that no one can see
into Her at all.
She's a place
of countlessness,
countless curvings and swellings
and buddings and pulsings,
growing and growing,
bursting
through sidewalks,
steeples,
reception lines,
contracts and vows,
those crusts
that mess
up so many beds.

XVII.

I couldn't have dreamed this up
—to be diverted from the mirror
by another face,
to be taken away
on the mind of another life,
to be someone else
so true
because
of someone else so true,
and not for just a week or a year
till the first heat is gone,
but on and on,
never ending
even when change
tries to douse us,
even when loneliness
tries and tries
to blow us out. ■

from *Death Self*

I. Before the Past Happened

He could not tell
how his life should be.
He just knew it was wrong.

But what did it matter
when all around him
people, like forests,
were going up in smoke?

There was a freedom
in calamity
he had just begun to savor.

He was like that now:
a confection
turned into somebody's
longing for more.

II. Mother of Death

Just for yourself
you plucked me from school
on a wild, sunny day when I was six.

We sipped chocolate sodas.
We frolicked in our smiles.
I never knew
I wanted *anything* so much:

my movie star mother,
your beautiful lips,
the perfume of your wrists,
your eyes wanting mine.
Such sweet shock to be desired!

When you take me again
I will feel just the same.

III. Silver Lining

He could tell
the burnt edges
had not burned out.
An edge, smokeless and cold,
was advancing its black
rim around him.
No one else
felt a thing.
He didn't welcome it, exactly.
But he was relieved.
It was finally on its way
and well out of his hands.
His life had always been
escape mixed with waiting.

IV. Outer Spaces

The wall came down,
was tarnished away,

ridiculed into a heap,
a nothing
that became an opening,
an absence
that became a road.

All walls crumble,
all resistance breaks,
all force decays:
it's the way
that humor takes,
like faith and death
and justice,
always breaking free.

V. Stepping Forth

The future was there.
She could feel it
in herself: a free horizon,
intimate as inhalation.
"It's the trust
one brings to the day," she'd say.
"One must
step forth
into the blank of the future.
Even death,
even the flame
that just went out,
is there,
right ahead,

safe as the space
between every
next breath
and fully within our grasp."

VI. Walking on Water

Waiting all our lives,
we expect it to happen,
and keep on waiting
for it to happen
as we expect.
But it never appears
until it does,
until it's too late
to see it coming,
even when we know
it's on the way.
It is its nature
to take us by surprise,
when we are
most focused
on our lives.
Fast or slow,
it is ours
when we are most
barely our own,
like walking on water must be
as thought-less
as pulse.

VII. Ready to Begin

Clearing away the normal
patterns and wastes of my day.
I prepare to meet myself on the page,
to see what is there,
to know, through the words,
what was waiting for me.

Clearing the path
for the end to start,
one waits for what is
as one waits on creation.

VIII. The Whole Truth

I say to myself:
"As you walk,
or sit,
or run,
or write,
practice what it's like
to be all gone,
a non-self self,
a not-there there,
an absence where
who you are
and where you are
has no
again."

I say to myself:
"You are
that absence
as you are
this presence,
alive and dead at once,
a place and a no place,
like an opening in
a conscious thicket—
both its shape
and its space."

IX. Sympathetic Rapture

The great owl of death
seizes me by the breath,
covers me with her wings,
breaks my will with her kiss,
devours me like an eclipse.

In sympathy, I shudder,
releasing all resistance,
enfolded in her shadow,
in the night of her body's shade.

As prey, I have no choice.
In moonlight, though,
as a lover letting go, I am all hers,
cradled, embracing, all unafraid.

X. Free Unknowing

This unexpected
unfamiliarity
with myself,
does it mean
that even I
am more
than I can ever know?
If so, why not death,
—my life in death,
the death in my life—
might it not be
as full of more
as my unknowing
means less
than dust strands do
in the cosmos at large?
It is God's joy, is it not,
that there is
eternally more to know?

XI. No Performance

Afraid to start,
afraid to fail,
I procrastinate
at learning
how to die,
even though I know

the fulfillment of my life
is told
in how relaxed I am
with death
at the center of my life.

To die as I was born,
with no intention,
moving out beyond, at any time
—what's the difference
between babies and the wise?
Only that the one
could *choose*
to be so freely given.

XII. Sunday in Los Chavez

In need of myth,
the human gods
just cloudy fossils of ideas,
I see new hope
in a tall tree row,
a tidal swell of green
that is the scene
of rendezvous,
the back wall of time,
a place behind
the scenery of the hours,
the backdrop prop
of the theater of my fears.

That cliff of trees,
of dream trees
sprouting up from twilight,
it greets me every Sunday
as I hang out the wash,
formal as death,
a landscape like a holy self
that is divine
with nothing more behind it,
not a god of deeds and duties,
just a place
normal as breath,
as mind,
as this and that,
or whatever
is behind us
and ahead.

XIII. Letting Go

How can I befriend the death
of anyone I love
unless I do to theirs
what I have done to mine?

Their lives just happened to me.
They were never my possession.
Their deaths were always free ahead.
The pain I feel for them is sheer fatigue:
Their deaths outline my dying,

and my life despises letting go.
Even though I know
there's nothing final but the past,

I can't submit
to freedom that's ahead
while bound, denying freedom
to the dead.

XIV. Death the Mentor

It is useless to do
what I am not,
useless
not to choose,
living like a ball
rolling down a table.

I must do my life
as I will do my death
—in mortal candor,
without timing or turning back,
a free finality in every act.

If I live like that
then death becomes an action
not a subjugation, and I am

no martyr to the ironies of time
but free as the hours

piercing through me,
free as death is free
of lies and fear and barter.

XV. Again and Again

That's what they mean
by "waking up,"
by "dying to who you are"
—that's Death Self,
the guide,
the way into being
alive as you die,
day after day,
living your death
with every breath,
timeless and ending,
beginning and gone.

Fear dies
when death is alive,
when death wears life
like an edgeless light.
That's why
the now never dies
when death is your guide
for fear's not there
to divide it.

XVI. No Gain

Achieving peace,
having success,
gaining advantage,
acquiring goodness
by grace or deeds
—how sad.
Having good
means having bad,
acquiring loss,
gaining reversal,
achieving the bitter end.
Settle for nothing,
it doesn't add up,
can't be subtracted.
It's the perfect point
—so true
you can't even want it.

XVII. Death Is the Rest

Making room in your mind
for life without your mind

closed shut,
allowing all you are

to see you
where you are,

you feel the free light
behind you

is inside you,
sensing Death,

Mind, the Divine,
are all the same.

What's in a name?
Death is the rest.

Open up, give it room,
let it breathe

the fear right out of you;
it is what's left of you;

it *is* you, free of you,
knowing you

like the truth
you know

when laughing
overcomes you. ■

Nine Eleven:
It's Always the Same:
Nothing Will Ever Be the Same
[12 September 2001 to 23 September 2001]

12 September 2001

We're lucky not to be one of them yet,
the vaporized,
who became
atmospheric,
their fifteen seconds of fame
spread like volcanic dust around the globe,
blocking reflection;
we've always been lucky.
Even now we have death
with our pleasures,
death to make the customers
happier to buy great quilts, log hammocks,
polar tech pouches, joy stick distractions.
But we know
what it means.

"Death plucks my ear
and says, 'Live,
I am coming,'" Virgil wrote,
turning his face from the porno squeals
of the killing fields
of the circus.
Death, you are here already,
our only way out,
our worst possible fear,
fast or slow, a sudden
closure, cauterizing life,
a long, thoughtful
agony that can't
be withstood for a second,
ripped from sunshine and our holy toys,
like arms torn off in a combine.

13 September 2001

It's always different,
now more than always.
The birds *are* the same,
but we've
mutated,
primates with venomous teeth,
thoughts like actual poison.
Our women don't mind
"collateral damage,"
"so heinous was the crime."
Our men like the idea
of anonymous slaughter.
We've used up the horror words.
We haven't run out of life, but we have
run out of our snotty disdain
for sweet illusions.
Now we're like everyone else,
caught between gallantry,
knee quaking, and tears
that no matter what
won't come loose.

14 September 2001

The bullies, the bigots,
the monkeys insane
with fear, ennobled
by its only
known over-the-counter
antidote—rage.
The mob thinkers,
the ruthless who
follow their own
rules, the thugs
in knight's clothing,
the self-righteous
sure as guillotines
are sure of gravity,
those with feasible morality,
who war has given
permission to abandon
with menacing calm
all distinction,
—do not join them, do not join them,
do not join them.

16 September 2001

Is it true
that anyone's cruelty
is wrong,
that wrong means
worthless results?
Why is it?
Because what works
feels like the right key
for a lock that has to be opened.
Cruelty jams all locks,
so nothing can close
forever.

16 September 2001

Horror abates.
Scars as scars remain.
Bullies find pulpits
for finery and shame.
The dead line up.
They lay no blame.
In death they can see
what we never see.
In death they cry out
stay alive,
stay alive,
"you must
love one another
or die."

17 September 2001

Humbled by Auden's view of us
as Eros and as Dust,
I have no graceful phrases;
my lyre is out of tune
dropped from a cradle
into a bog.
Auden's right.
We must choose between canyons of corpses
and patient, heartbreaking,
endlessly abrading give and take,
the polishing, slow motion torture
to be with the world
and each other
as lovers are
laughter loving,
in fathomless complicity
so all complaint
is dust
on the mirror of erotic trust.

21 September 2001

He's been reduced
to two parts of himself:
the cockeyed
flatterer of fate,
and the intellectual sniper
sighting down the barrel,
not quite wide awake,
a half full guy, half empty
locked in the trunk of a junk truck,
an accurate skeptic,
a man
with his finger
on the filament
tied to the hair trigger
of the future
to detect
the slightest
wobble,
tremble,
tautness
on the verge of a plummeting
explosion
in the minds of those who've awakened
to their exclusion
from the world,
to what the powerful
drunk minds
consider good and true.

22 September 2001

We are falling out of the world
as we know it
like people jumping from fire
a hundred floors up,
free falling with more
hope in the space between fire
and the mush of their fatal thuds
than just waiting to be
cooked up
like overdressed chops.
You just
have to do something
everyone says,
anything really, anything
but wait for the end,
helplessly frozen.
Jump,
it's a short-term solution,
like dropping bombs,
suicidal too,
in the long run,
but perhaps
the only and happiest
thing to do
when nothing's to be done. ■

Elective Carnage
[Iraq: 20 March 2003 to 9 April 2003]

I.

It's not seditious to want
a life without inspection,
interrogation, and demands
for definition.
"If you don't have something to hide"
why worry about
spies in your soup,
your hair, your bum?
Secrecy, come on,
you know this,
"it's none of your business."
Being forced to describe
a privacy
in public terms
when no terms at all will do,
being forced to endure
your innocent life
described by the law,
means getting caught
for nothing at all, defiled
by fill-in-the-blank suspicions.

IV.

Sanity peels up,
laminate unglues,
seams spread, warping

cracks the seals, and sometimes
clean socks
are the final
refuge; sometimes
it's two,
clean,
perfect lines of verse,
as hard to come by
as peace, as catching
Fat Man falling
before he explodes.

V.

Rivets are popping
out of the missiles,
the subs, the drones,
the battle tanks;
soldiers are frying up beetles,
sipping antifreeze
to stop the pain,
dogs and cats
have been decoding
secret orders all along,
sniffing out
their demonic
randomness
and getting everything
adorably wrong.
But the missiles
falling apart in mid flight
now that's something

even the snails
are applauding
in their silent,
charmed,
vulnerable joy.

VI.

Could it be we've triggered
the whole, horrible
booby trap dream again,
another cycle of Hell's
ingenuity, another run
of the butcher girls
crooning death songs,
prepping to skin
the whole world alive?
What a tune,
that high-pitched sizzle
of death's little angels
in grimy dresses
and blood-caked stares
—we can hear them
cawing
their baby lisp laugher,
torch songs from the last
slaughter, now
settling for another,
like an orphan might think
a buzz saw is its mother.

VIII.

Some people won't
sink in fear, refusing
to drown
in vats of adrenaline fire.
Some people
tip the vats over,
and gingerly
walk away,
gingerly,
gingerly
walk away
into another
way of seeing.
They don't
give horror its due.
They see it as just
one more grain
on the most
beautiful beach
under Aphrodite's
smooth, cool feet.

IX.

Geese and cranes are going north,
elms are infant green,
just enough rain
so the mustard glows all over the ground.
This is here.
It's the same war everywhere.

Over there, Rachel Corrie
was crushed to death
by a bulldozer and its driver
who ran over her and then
backed over her again,
turning her bones
into jagged wet dice
in the bruised bag of her body.
This morning, I am at peace
in my office under the reading lamp
in a warm robe,
and Rachel Corrie,
who thought peace was right,
is twenty-three for eternity,
a girl with a spine
and no skeleton to speak of.

XIV.

Sleepless again,
trees uprooting themselves,
flowers wilting on purpose,
snails heating up in the sun
to boil with accusative
self-immolation.
It's just as we thought.
Nothing can stand
what has come to be.
We are at the beginning
of the end
of the dream
we've loved more

than we've feared
its horribly short life.
The cats refuse
to wash themselves,
or sharpen their claws
on the elms. Even
the lizards taunt them,
hoping against hope
they'll be eaten.

XVI.

Helpless faces
mobbing for food and water,
hating us who kill them,
feed them, torture them,
liberate and rend them,
rebuild them, cosmetically
enhance them, smack them
with Coke
and Winstons,
and scratch-and-sniff ads
on blow-ins
in piles of *Golf
Digests* and *Vogues*,
shrink wraps intact.
And who are we?
Are we them
by a tear
in the toilet paper walls of luck?
Are we waiting our turn,
not them

for now,
but always, forever them,
waiting,
disguised
in fate's
fatal,
tear-away attire?

XXIV.

It's either the muscle-bound
mercy killers
liberating the soon to be dead,
or the morally muscled nuns
vulnerable as sugar ants,
either soldiers of compassion
with stealth weapons
and Movie Tone ambitions
or lynx-like workers
pacifying the vengeful
and nursing the bereaved
and their paper thin children,
either the saintly militia
heroic with righteous swagger
or the young woman
who uses her body against the tanks.
Who do you admire?
Who do you want to admire you?
For which one
is admiration
a frivolity of power?
For which one

is frailty a weapon
beyond abuse?

XXV.

The war is over, they declare.
It's left the screen as fast
as depleted sitcoms disappear.
Combat, now, decidedly unsexy
no more news than a playground opening
or a not-quite-spectacular one car crash.
It's all still real, naturally.
The corpses, the funerals,
the shattered stores,
the mothers tearing their faces
in Arlington and Basra,
the dysentery, the babies drained,
the insane holding their eyes,
the land mines, live rounds waiting,
all invisible behind the reruns, super-
market walls of cereal and crackers,
the TV ads for shavers so sharp
they despoil sequoia forests on your chin,
and the grinning anchor dandies
squeezing in the body counts between
the sixth action weather update of the evening
and the twelve-second logo of tonight's
world minute news. ∎

Watching You Go

for my father

At 9255 Swallow Drive, Los Angeles

Watching you go
in your island garden above the smog,
    above the dazzling ruins
    rich with sauces, starry killers;

watching you go,
    an Ozymandias among his orchids,
the phantom pain of your absent lives
like your fingers, numb and jittery,
tugging at gray leaves, skin so dry
it skids across the bones;

watching you go,
    an object among your objects
    I visited all my life
    as a darling oddity,
        petted, even loved,
darting among the glamour,
never abandoned, never home;

watching you go,
alone with your fascinations,
your museum of temptations;

watching you go,
watching myself left behind, a subject
      tending to your taste, your place, your pyramid,
my cherished past erased again,
once again, for good;

watching you go,
I see myself emerge from you,
your sneer of cold command,
a guest no longer in your life,
      my old wings
      unpeeling in the Summer Time;

watching you go,
      as lonely as I always am,
a prince and a pauper
who never learned the trick;

watching you go
at last,
      like catching each day
of the Parthenon's decay
in a single glance or two.

Intoxication

Watching you go, old hero,
    Laertes in his Sunday suit
    planting in the mud,
        numb to the lies of his son,
the Odyssey half begun,
    his adventuring child admiring
    the casual folly of his fun;

watching you go, old hero,
sharks all around me
on the bow of the trawler, snapping for breath,
trapped like me;
    what were you thinking?—your face turned to the sea,
    so far away,
        sideburns feathering out like Hermes's wings
        from your old Greek captain's hat;

watching you go,
I remember Tijuana
when you hid
a lit Delicado
behind your back for me to puff
and I dragged deep,
    tempting fate: no longer just
    your prisoner kid, but now
    your accomplice, too,
        in marital misdemeanors:
    what joy to foil
    the sweet keeper
        as we teamed against her
        in happy vice;

watching you go,
your long ago scorn
     for my sloppy letters, Christmas wrappings,
     like squalls in dishpans,
     live wires in the tub,
your lightning eyes
drilling me to the floor
teaching me the fact of work:
     work true
     or be washed away
     in shame;

watching you go,
begging me,
     like bargaining for a pot or painting,
to show you mercy
and put you to sleep,
and then,
     like chewing the next bite,
     as if you'd said nothing at all, you say,
          "How marvelous the Titian show . . .
          if I could only go";

watching you go,
my feet still sore
from standing behind you
years ago for years,
     a porter for the great collector,
     bored numb by your endless fun,
relieved to be around
as your flycatcher's eye spots prey
in the Roman junk store a mile away;

watching you go,
our pride in each other
the same as it was
when we peed on Trajan's column
thirty-two years ago
when you were as old as I am now,
and I was twenty-one,
drunk on chocolate and dusk in the Piazza Navona,
drunk on being your son,
on being alone with you
drunk on being a father;

watching you go, old hero,
     cleaning your closets of the choicest ties,
     eyeing the rows of Brooks Brothers blue;
all that's left of you
I want, you wore,
and it's still too big for me;

watching you go,
I savor my bacon and eggs each morning with you
at the blue plate diner
by the pier when I was ten:
     the salty grease, the yokes, the toast and jam,
     this new discovery
     of how to eat and how to be—savoring
          every sense in every moment, even though
we could never do more than exclaim
the passing surface of our pleasures.

In the Ruins of Now

Watching you go,
I'm lost to the world
    in cloud-gray pebbles on the beach
    at the first low tide I've seen in twenty years,
free of fear to risk my pleasure,
    to risk being late, the shame of a minor trouble,
    forgetting to be miserable to keep you loving me;

watching you go,
I feel night drain
into me like ink,
    like ink swirls, gulping ink,
    hot ink, sweet ink, ink shine,
        ink all over my teeth, all over the sky,
ink bubbling from the wound,
ink clouds forming from the paper cuts,
    hissing ink;

watching you go,
the terrible rainy days already here,
    the dark woods of rain,
    torrential foliage of the trees,
    skies dense as concussions,
        lightning closer than forgetting;

watching you go
in the shadows of birds and flowers,
of feet and hands,
of pencils on paper in bright noon light,
    in the shadows of sanity and deception, of dark desire,
        cold-blooded shadows,

        shadows of family, of marriage, of escape,
        the honest shadows of bewildered lives;

watching you go,
unable to explain to you
what I mean when I say
we are known by what we love;

watching you go,
unable to explain to you
my thrill at finding lilies frescoed on the mud of Knossos,
     rising from a green "calyx of leaves,"
finding them in a picture book not ten minutes after
planting Lilies of the Valley,
     a sentimental flower of my mother,
unable to explain to you
coincidence so sublime:
     potential flowers in the ground,
        virtual flowers on the wall,
     our virtual potential
     never, finally, met;

watching you go,
I relive my disappointments,
scrubbing away their stains
     like working for weeks to make the saucepan bright as new;
        but some little dents and nicks
        will never get clean
        and I wonder:
Is that one of those truths
     or just me
     being lazy as accused?

The Elephants' Graveyard

Watching you go,
waiting for the cut to heal
so another cut can take its place,
another scar can scar a scar;

watching you go,
I hear screams from streets
        fifty years ago, tomorrow, last week,
screams behind the fan whirl,
        the white noise of art,
screams behind rebellion's
insect life of flame
—no change, no death, can mute a scream;

watching you go,
I wait it out,
        holding on to you,
your grip and mine
aching to release,
        knowing as I know
        nothing will change
        when you're gone,
the same sorrow,
salted with delight,
healing over with sorrow
over and over
until, for you,
        then me,
there is no night;

watching you go,
I know what must be done:

live now
     as if without you
     while you're here,
as I live now without my death
while it's on the way,
     live as if without the loss to come,
         with the loss already known,
     slipping into a sinkhole in the yard,
     sipping gimlets in a deck chair, debonair;

watching you go,
I see the bodies in their heaps and piles,
     the bulldozered cords
     of legs, of trunks,
         the tornados of their eyes,
all the grief in the world:
a universal fog, a fatal sauna
rising up in a hiss of soot
over the elephants' graveyard;

watching you go,
I can't comprehend what happens to the pain after we feel it; does it
bleed
     into the underground mind of the age?;
         are there great plumes of pain
         polluting the conscious stream
         in Biafra, Salvador, Wounded Knee, Siberia?;
     are symphonies played
     on the bars of all our cages?;

watching you go,
nothing changes
but the change of something
which never changes.

Forgotten Spy

Watching you go,
I understand my secrets,
        why nobody knows who I am altogether,
                why nobody could
                make sense of all the parts,
why I am so stealthy, stone faced, uncatchable;
I understand how much of me now
is all about not being you,
        not being my image of you
        caught in the image you have of yourself
                while dressing so smartly, tying your ties
                in the mirror of all their eyes;

watching you go
dream dancing to "Oklahoma,"
        snoozing off in your Harley Davidson chair,
        jolting up, off and on, to a happy strain,
                croaking out "Oh What a Beautiful Morning"
unrestrained,
all the misery of our life,
        the hood of your scars and sorrows,
                the hood of *their* eyes,
unable to mute for a moment
your welcoming of the world;

watching you go,
I water my garden
in the twilight, watering with you,
        ghost not gone,

watching water rise in the beds
as you have done on endless late afternoons,
> our common bond
> an impatience not unlike devotion;

watching you go,
I feel your shyness
closed as stone,
> not anger, not punishment to fit
> no one's crime,
>> just your terror of embarrassment—
it's not your fault,
> even if I knew the pain
> of hugging shiny armor on a sunny day;
plumping your pillows, holding you up to take a pee,
> tenting the covers over your feet,
I wait all day for your smile,
> not for your approval, but
>> for the reason you suffered all the glare,
>> all the possible humiliation
>> with such pride before their eyes
—I wait for your undisguised pleasure in being
a happy old Scrooge McDuck
sharing all his incredible stuff.

Better Than Nothing

Watching you go,
we descend through opal cloud seas
to the bottom of the sky,
      down to the riches of bottom-feeders
      steaming at the roots of your island above smog
where you inhale the mists, heaving for a decent breath,
but never far from a laugh at anyone's expense;

watching you go,
      wanting to serve your needs
      after a life of dodging
      the service of your interests;
what's the difference
if the fear's the same?;

watching you go,
a steroid high putting spring in your hinges,
you show a gymnast's grace,
      shifting bedsores to a cooler place,
a jock of survival, a champion hanger-on,
the performance is still
all that matters
—anything, thank God, for fun;

watching you go
through one false spring after another,
      laughing it up with you
      at casket jokes on sitcoms stupid
            as pulling on your pants with your shoes still on,
            me on my knees tugging at your cuffs, the impatient kid who'd do
anything to please;

watching you go,
I regress to ancient traumas,
but I am not intent on making you wince
each time I stutter all day over Ss;
I don't want you to wonder why
     and dutifully take the blame
     for faults you can't find anymore because
     I threw them all away
        so we'd both
        never have to;
so much of what's yours is mine;

watching you go,
     abandoned, shipwrecked on your shadow,
I hear you wanting to leave, but not
going without
the desire to stay,
     your life seeping out without you
     while you stay tuned
     an innocent at eighty-three, omnivorous for any treat;

watching you go
as you tell us of "tearing up"
three times, you said, at "visual things,"
     at paintings you're stumped you can't remember
—only the memory of sentiment
is cherished enough to be retold,
     the sentiment you dreaded like frost dreads dawn.
Have you become like me:
     that what you reject
     you come to at the end

—or has that
been you
     in me
all along?
Watching you go,
we wait on you, washing and driving,
     focused servants for a while,
          undignified and free with feeling;
it's the least we can do
when I can't really see you
through the ice curtain
     of our habits and the haze
     of your pains clouding up
     from my mouth in a veil
     of unspoken shock;

watching you go,
I will never
put myself in the cripple's box
     to be stunted for show again,
I will never choose
     what was before you learned
     to die so strong and kind;

watching you go,
your greatest gift to me
is now
I hope
I go like you,
     not your misery
     but how you pay your respects
          each moment among your agonies, reaching
     for what's always out of reach,

     never turning away from a chance
to let your pleasure be a sacrifice,
never missing a gift to notice and approve,
a foolishness to notice and annihilate,
      giving all you've got
      in praise or mockery;

watching you go,
I never wanted to be who you are,
      a variation on a theme;
I didn't want to live like you
      in an ocean of clouds, so free to be so unhappy,
but now I'd be honored
to be like you,
      never turning your back on the day,
      swimming up through the clouds
      holding your breath,
      passing us all
         to the top and over. ■

The Owl, the Seal, and the Coyotes

—October 1993

Watching you go through the last days,
I tell you once that "you're my hero," and you,
        barely able to breathe,
instantly reply,
        like a Don cleaning his nails,
"Watch out for the goddamn accountants."

Watching you go,
I recognize the final photos of your life.
        What a scream!
Flat on your back,
        in your ratty, flamingo-pink tee and horrible robe,
        oxygen tubes in your nose,
you sensed the camera, and raised your arms over your head,
a mock ballerina, toe-dancing off the screen.

Watching you go,
I hear on the phone that you're gone,
        and tell my sister by phone that you're gone,
        that you took all day,
                holding the shepherdess by the hand,
that you left around 6:00 p.m.,
wearing a long blue cloak and a tickled grin,
        two flappers by your side,
eager for the night to begin,
        as always, wanting
        what happens next.

Watching you go,
I see, amazed,
the gray cottonwood limbs
blossom into a twilight owl, huge
 like the tree,
 its black feathered bark
 disguising the promise that trees can fly,
like you can do the impossible
and finally die.

Watching you go,
I turn nasty.
I snap at idiot questions,
made desperate
 by a mute
 suffocation
 of love
  by bile,
 of loss
  by relief,
 of privacy
  by violation,
  by undesired
  nudity
  and no place to hide.
You can't
just say no
to the rape of the press.

Watching you go,
I feel so little yet,
 mostly a sadness
 over the absence of feeling;

I want so much to miss you;
I can hear the hollow roll
     of rubber tires on polished wooden floors
     move toward my life even now,
the sound of your scooter,
moving you on
past disease
to one more breakfast out of bed.

Watching you go on the wine dark sea,
I think of Odysseus,
     brine caked, awaking on Nausicaa's shore;
"wine dark"
is not the color only,
it is more
the dark, intoxicating surface
of the speechless deep.

Watching you go
out to sea with your pals,
I look over at the empty chair on the boat
to see if you're OK,
     if it's all too much,
     if you're reaching for the out of reach,
if you're reaching for me
to reassure me
     —but you're not.

Watching you go
in a trail of roses on the sea,
     your ashes falling like a pure white wish
     through the muscle of the waves,
        your planter's hat riding the breakers to be,

    I wonder if Proteus,
   nudging a baby seal
   so it pops up and down
   through the sad bouquet,
was sending a message from you.
I conclude
that I can't read the signs,
but the token will do.

Watching you go,
   feeling so little of you,
I see now
the performance of your life,
   never having been allowed before
   behind the curtain:
You liked to make us happy;
   it was safer when we were having fun.

Watching you go,
   the swarms of your fame
   inhaled up my nose,
   sticking like gnats to my lips and tongue,
I wave them off with my cap,
   as they blow away
   to the next famous death.

Watching you go
through a perfect winter twilight in the mountains,
   just as the sun inched down
   and finally dropped
   into the dark,
     like your breath inched out
     and stopped
     as you dropped out of view,

we heard coyotes bark and laugh,
    relieved of light
    like you, when life was lifted from you,
then sensed them
tense and watch,
    I swear it's true,
your easy disappearance
moving through the night. ∎

A Christmas Dream*

for Vincent Leonard Price Jr., 1911–1993

> *"... to enter into death with open eyes."*
> *"... to extend the human heart to life's full measure."*
> —Marguerite Yourcenar

Sinatra and Bing a-caroling,
a Hollywood December rain,
     kid lights glazed
          through clerestories in the sugared fog

—and you, ol' boy, just there,
peeking out behind a Eucalyptus tree,
     a rude Virgil

grinning with an infant's squint of glee,
telling us to come along,
to pretend that we are dead, like you,
     and go around the world as if we had no life to lose,

as if we'd lost it all already,
         all that we adored, but had
         one last chance to see it, timelessly,

for as long as we could feel it.
And so you take me by the hand
and tell me stories through the night.
We go to Rome, bathe our feet in cold white wine,

smooth the Venus of Cyrene's holy slopes,
fish the coast off Malibu,
watch ourselves together in Paris windowpanes,

light sweet smokes in Tijuana bars.
Then at London you veer off
and I go home, running through the bosque in the Spring,
past Jemez ponds, Los Chavez midnights and their stars, and come

to booths in old cafes and talking tables,
and, to you,
   friends of my heart,
   each one,
   your names like breath
   keeping me calm and wide awake,
even when pretending in his final game.

I can't fake it, though, for long
playing that I'm dead. Love without desire
is pure fun for you, old man, mortal work for me.

But just at the edge of sleep, as I awake,
   you, yourself, your little soul,
     peeks out again behind the tree,
and as I reach for you, you move,

as always, out of reach,
and I feel you wink and smile and wave me off
as you drop a postcard from Ravenna in the sand;

in your sculptured hand it reads:
"Dear Boy,
Morpheus, divine god,
had me for a while.

But how clear I've been
     since I awoke last week from life.
You know how I am, light as ever, always giving late advice.

It's all about your open eyes. Just live
as if you were long gone like me,
     say yes and yes and yes again, say wholly yes,
as if each moment were

the sweetest memory of your life.
    When all
        is said and done, dear boy,
            the duty

gods like best
    is fun.

          love, Dad" ■

---

*"May it please the One who perchance is to expand the human heart to life's full measure."
—inscribed on the grave marker of Marguerite Yourcenar, 1903–1987, author of *Memoirs of Hadrian*.

"Little soul, gentle and drifting . . . one moment still, let us gaze together on these familiar shores, on these objects which doubtless we shall not see again. . . . Let us try, if we can, to enter into death with open eyes."
—from the final paragraph of the *Memoirs of Hadrian*.

—with special gratitude to Angelique Cook Wilcox who took the journey.

Fortune's Child

—August 30, 1996

Now that you're gone,
I watch myself starting to go,
frantic not to seem old,
embarrassed by my embarrassment.
But sprinting across the street on my morning hike today,
    avoiding commuters and high-school drivers,
I knew who I was at last:
"fortune's child" as you said,
your child,
recklessly happy,
remembering you
    still impressed
    by pleasure
    the week before you died.
Even then
you hadn't lost
your fool-
hardiness
for fun,
    sneaking off,
    chauffeured,
    for a cappuccino
    miles from your bed,
    for a wheelchair roll
    through a farmer's market,
    sniffing tomatoes,
    thumping melons,

    hungry for turnips,
      hot garlic and butter.
The audacity of pleasure-
seeking
so close to the end,
    barely able to breathe,
    still game,
    still anything goes.
That's who you are to me
now that you're dead.

No matter how
miserable I feel,
    how crippled,
    how depressed,
    you felt,

I know your will
to praise
by being pleased
overrode prognosis
time and again
for the most
banal and exalted ends:
    orchid blossoms, oatmeal,
    an easy shit.

That must be why this morning
I remembered you
    still young in me,
    still moving free
    through the garden of dawn,
springing across the asphalt,
as I followed you
this once,
this time,
to this
sweet place
of being
with you now
    as if there never was
    any difference between us. ■

from *Lost Gardens*

Moonlight Park

for Susie Morrow, who named the park when she was three

In the garden of croquet
      on the public lawn of the park
—across from the house with acanthus leaves
      where Susie lives, in Corinthian grace,
the myth of her childhood, her classical youth,
      as mother of dollies and daughter of doting friends—
we played together all afternoon, us and the kids,
      in melon-cool breezes on sunny grass, sober as larks,
thunderheads frowning in foreign thoughts
      too far from home to bother.

How can I say how I felt?
    I felt like the dream of a man
asleep in a myth
    on trustworthy nights beneath the moon,
a dream as calm as an optimist's fears,
    without so much as a spark
from acetylene streets
    tearing down the darkness while we're asleep,
a utopian dream so real
    the dreamer is convinced he's wide awake
in a dream so safe the forbidden is a bore
    and nothing's ever lost
for there is no way
    to fall from grace
when Eden's just a place
    to play croquet. ■

Twentieth-Century Spring

How sweet to have lived in this froth of TVs,
of Frigidaires, Hondas, Hersheys, PCs,

this hiss of fun foaming up from our age,
up from the rolling loam of our skulls,

the skulls of so many fellows from so many slaughters,
of so many mothers and daughters and sons, that they seem

like a topsoil of talcum, a dust bowl of death's heads,
quaking on meadows of lime green Jello. ■

Monet Is Not at Giverny

In your yellow dining room,
     your black-eyed Susan dining room
          with its sunflower chairs and dishes,
          its buttercup cupboards,
          the honey pollen pattern of its floor,
in your noon-light, daisy field of a room,
     years before I was born,
you lived so clearly
who you are
that now I see
     all my life
     I've wanted to feel just as I did
     when I saw the wild meadow of your dining room
          for the first time
and imagined how I'd feel
to be remembering
     how I learned to listen at your table,
     intimate as if
     in a rolling field
     of tall grasses in a breeze,
          awed by the delicate
          motion of ideas, the flowering
          of comfort,
          of indulgence and conversation.

Now I've known
the real Giverny
without you there.
It was not as true
as the myth I'd made of it,

a mere museum
     magnificent with its postcard views,
     botanical trinkets,
until I saw,
     at an open window,
a white dove floating through the blossoms
like a gull skimming waves
and I felt the breezes blowing back
the white slip of a curtain,
     like sea wind on feathers,
showing me a cloud-flowered,
     yellow density of daisies,
     the rainbows of your hollyhocks
remembered
as I would
imagine them.

And I will always confuse
what I know of you
with what I want of you,
     great, bearded, sunny Santa of springtime.
The light between us,
     light of the life urge
     pouring though my nerves
     as it flows through your flowers, your trees, your vines, the light
between us glows
through my brain,

remembering the dove,
the slip of windy curtain
ruffling shade
through conversations
we have never had
that I recall
    like a myth
    that used to be
    just what happened
    in a given moment on a given day
that's now forgotten
    like the sun on your face
    one Sunday
        while you feel the sun
        on your face
            on Monday. ■

Monet's *The Seine at Giverny*
The National Gallery, Washington, D.C.

Those lazy trees
by the river at Giverny,
the sane river flowing,
mirroring the day,
nothing more, or less,
than where it is.

The river never stays, but the same
reflection is in it all the time in the painting.
And all the time that summer of 1897
the real water moved like thoughts
through the day
with trees on its mind. ■

Seeing the Obvious

[*in memoriam*: the Montano Road cottonwood,
        cut down for a useless bridge in December 1995]

Outside the kitchen window on a sleepless night,
        I see that the deluge of bark
                on the endless cottonwood tree in the garden
                        is so much more than me
                                I have to move my head
to move my eyes across it.
        It takes the same surprising effort
                to believe
                                the changes that I see
                                are more
than my feelings.
        So I move my whole self to the ditch shore grasses,
                rich in willows, nightshade, black-eyed Susans,
                        the deep-sea ocean grass of weeds
                                swaying in the aromatic skies
for miles of walking
        through the backlands near the river,
                moving my whole self down deep arcades
                        of hidden passageways of trees, serene
                        as wind eddies far
from lightning in the west.
        These paths of curiosity and high repose,
                I move along
                        in foresight,
                                which feels too much

like memory,
>> are murdered now
>>> by herbicides and highways.
>>>> As surely
>>>>> as I will die,

all the ditch weeds and their blossoms,
>> the yellow primrose moon weeds, rag weeds, morning glories,
>>> nettles, tumbleweeds and creepers,
>>>> all will be
>>>>> deprived of their nature
as a wilderness inside
>> the regimented glade
>>> of exiled city space.
>>>> This garden's past,
>>>>> which is right now,
is as lost
>> as the music singers played
>>> to Homer's words
>>>> in a time that might as well have never been,
>>>>> so covered up it is in stories, lies,
revisions, and the blankness of forgetting.
>> So with my life of days
>>> and meals and mornings,
>>>> books and talk
>>>>> and all sweet and cool and mellow
times
so dense I don't remember
>> more than a day or two of it,
>>> only
>>>> that it all has been.
>>>>> So here I am on the ditch bank,

this floating garden of weeds and worlds
 about to be bulldozed
  for a bridge,
    not the whole garden razed
     just its
invisible integrity,
 its economy of place
  replaced like wisps of grasses
    changed
     into indiscriminate fire.
And there is nothing I can do
 but see the garden
  as a lover would
    in the only seconds left,
     seeing to preserve in sight
what no one
 will have known
  to remember,
    moving my whole self
     so at least
I will be
 more than me,
  me plus the world plus my effort
    —love is never
     a total waste. ∎

Oxford Thames

Feeding crumbs to fowl
from a backyard on the Thames,
    a twentieth century
    American poet,
        without tenure,
        workshop,
        pedigree,
        cult or coven,
    useful
    as a crossbow stringer,
    a master of the two-man saw,
somewhere in the far
outback of my life,
    the arduous
    Interior,
happy to be
the best
risk I can take,
    a forest floor
    of poems behind me,
the old motives
of glorious
re-cognition
in other minds
discredited,
    I feel myself to be
    cleansed at least
    of importance,
        no more
        lonely
        for old dreams
        than I would be

                for old lovers
                who were more
                numb pain
                than startling pleasure,
            a creature among creatures,
          weed among weeds,
    a part of the feeding life
    of mallards and coots and all the Queen's swans,
                a human monkey
                conscious of trying
                to be what he is,
    superfluously just
    to birds of a feather,
                tossing crumbs to the runts
                and bill-battered bums
    who have made it so far
    just fine
    without
    my compassion,
                without
                my loneliness for
                the soft
                crutch of usefulness
                I'm tossing away
                to be free
                just so
    I can say my way
                around
                and through
                and into
                the truth
                I can see
    with all
    that's left of me. ■

In the Parlor of the Tuileries

In the parlor of the Tuileries,
the ordered rows of chestnut trees,
    so royal
      their leaves
      drop up
        into the sky,
give a cemetery feel
of dense hilarity.

The black trunk pillars of the trees,
     machinery straight,
make a jail of leafy green
arranged like the dead in my head,
     madcap, dead
       by their own hands
        or the fuss of chance.

It's a nursery
of old friends in here,
     death's trimmed hedge
     growing like flagpoles
        sprouting crosses,
        crowns of thorns,

tears pouring through
sad regiments
of sovereign wood,
    so full of pain
      the rain falls like the last
      ending of a laugh,
         like the gray
         flustering
         of pigeons in the dusk,
               the calamities of feathers,
               the purrings of erotic mess,
death's joke
washing down
    through the template of the trees,
    washing away solemnity. ■

The Rock at Schoodic Point, Acadia National Park

for Rini

Either or,
the fatal

choice,
are words,

are finite sounds,
not prophecies,

local maps
of local thoughts

that pass and change
like one and two

become the stage
of holy wars

important
as sparks

extinguished
in puddles.

And
is

the grammar
of reality.

On Schoodic Point
everything is and,

is all at once—
rock, tides, gulls,

blossoms
in crevices

tight as blades;
and you and I

wrapped around each other
on the stone

in exultation,
with our grief,

our hollowness,
our hard,

cold
joy,
the tender rock
within us

bared,
the illusion

of sense,
of making sense,

breaking apart
in the weather

with no warning
but acceptance

of everything
all at once.

Even the waves
come all at once

in a line
one after another

until the once
we are

is over
and the waves move through

where we have been,
inevitable

as they will be
just once themselves

when what they are
is over. ■

The Woods

My new office,
    the latest of secret places,
        of dens beneath floorboards,
        sitting rooms hidden in attics,
        caves of work
        disguised as apartments,
        backyard lairs in nests of trees,
my new office,
    with its white pine floors, and white
    terraces of beautiful books,
floats above
a ghostland
where an elm grove used to stand
    that I cut down
    to make room for myself.
The elms are still in my mind,
those weed trees
    that proliferate
    their leaves
    even as logs,
        that refuse
        to be timber,
        too used to living
            —like me
            at fifty-five, refusing
            to be done.

This "woods" of mine, now,
    this forest
    of all the ideas I can find,
is the last place, perhaps, that I'll make
to hide myself
so I can be
what others might need of me,
if they can find me,
    so I can serve
    without being cut down
    for other purposes,
        where I can be
        worth my effort
        as all things in this world
                are worth their effort
                until they can give no more. ■

In the *Meadow* with Sisley

at the National Gallery, Washington, D.C.

All around us:
windy flower grasses, scent-
rivers steaming, tree
shade washing over light, the world
gone to its profusion,
whole oceans in a single leaf,
squalls waiting in weed stalks,
hurricanes gathering in seeds;
everywhere, a wild sea mistfog
breezing through smoky rooms.

The day in that painting,
called *Meadow*, as one might call a daughter,
could live itself out
on tenement middens with rooftop gardens,
on waveless beaches with ripples paved in stone,
on sandpaper mesas
polishing lungs to a strange luminescence
not wholly unlike a house far away in the rain,
glowing yellow, crackling in the kitchen
with aromas of the wilderness
civilized as wild fields are
wet
and unbroken
in the high
drawing rooms
of the flat,
desiccate
prisons of Art. ■

Round Rocks

for a sick friend

You asked
what the round rocks
        in my pocket might mean
        or was it just "Why?"
        I can tell you they are
evidence
of the possible
        even
        in the field
        of randomness,
even in the lost eons of the waves:
even there
        circles can be made.
        Even in the gore and tears
        of all our idiot wars
something perfect
might be rounded out,
        not that I believe
        it's us,

but something
we're not apart from,
        something we belong to
        like sand belongs to
waves,
        our whole species
        as inconspicuous
as a lumpy rock
never, it might seem,
fit for a circle
. . . but given time,
given other rocks beside it,
given time. . . . ■

The Earned Impossibility

for my father and mother

Nursing expensive water
in a virtuoso Parisian hotel,
    I'm self-consciously not
swank enough for the French
bankers and matrons perched,
    tails curled around them, on soft sofa seats.
So I could feel you both settling in
poshly rumpled, smiling foolish love smiles at me,
    your son, a cameleon of comfort, sweating to be
punctually at ease,
smiling at my dead zealotry
    to sample but not succumb
to patrician perfections
designed to make myself feel
    as different from you to myself
as you looked to me all my life
as voluptuous paragons
    lost for awhile in each other's eyes.

Now that I see a fool in the mirror
more foolish than you,
  I have earned the impossible
pleasure of not
being able to judge you.
  Yes, I know how I feel about you,
about your daredevil lives,
your copious failings,
  your show-off pleasures
at the expense of my own.
But judging can't be done anymore by me
  if I wish to save myself
from my own poison glance.
I thank the muses for this impossibility,
  and leave you to yourselves
as a convert softly
leaves the old gods
  behind. ■

Stratigraphy in the Luxembourg Gardens

We live upon
layers of hours.

No place exists
where the past hasn't been.

A humus of moments
makes up our world.

So, padding along on our old sore feet
on gravel paths through chestnut groves, sycamores,

copper beeches, past espaliered apple trees and ivy
swags
soothing our eyes on the curvy, eternal

epiphany of sex
rocking the stone bodies

of shameless lovers
in the fountains of the Luxembourg Gardens,

it's possible to hear Sartre and Beauvoir
arguing ethics, clawing the ground,

generosity and morality
making converts of each other,

and on the next layer below
to hear

the crunch of jackboots
as Nazi generals stroll

and take their ease from hunting Jews
and humiliating the French.

The Luftwaffe headquartered Goring,
and his tons of imperial brocade,

in the Luxembourg when I was five
an ocean away, fifty-one years ago.

The Nazis kept the paradise park
pristine of course,

and disciplined even the gayest bouquets
to behave like sprays

of freezing lead.
One can feel a certain triumph

walking through blossoms now
with the Nazi past

so many layers below,
and feel a hot joy at the gross

unlikelihood
of storm troopers

grabbing us by the ankles
and pulling us down to Hell.

We are so
far out of reach

of the past
we forget

the present
grows up from it,

that it nurtures anything
that comes along,

especially old weeds
like hate

that slip through the layers,
choke out the now,

and become a present
that no one believes

could ever have happened,
unless

they had actually felt
long before

the same roots themselves
gagging their minds,

growing to fill
their mouths,

their eyes,
their whole heads

with luxuriant horror
that no one believed,

even when it smothered
what they most loved,

even as it shoved
their own hands

like devilish roots
down the throat of a horrified other. ■

Vita Umbratiles

"Life in the shade,"
that's all the sane really want:
to be out of sight, off to one side, unseen from the road,
egos content
with breezes and peaches
and speech with no need
for furtive encoding
and fugitive speed.

That's what Virgil wanted from his talent,
to be out of the reach
of the great pax master,
the divine, vile Augustus,
that Cosmic force in a toga,
a gravity even the muse couldn't deflect.

So Virgil squeezed
his perfections slowly,
writing praises that took
eternities of shade
to voice all the grays.

Virgil gardened and wrote,
wrote and gardened,
so far from Rome
he'd rarely be told
to think half truths
and to trust half truths enough to say them.

An escape
artist, master of shadows
he tied his own
knots and slipped
free from the peace that he praised,
the noose of his own
shady cunning,
that peace
enforced
down the throats of the grateful. ■

Being No One, Someplace

for Jim Rini

If you uprooted yourself from your life,
you could come to a public place,

the Luxembourg Gardens in Paris, let's say,
and spend every day there until you die,

sunning yourself by the pond,
making poems while lovers

make spoons with each other on benches nearby, and never
make the acquaintance of anyone, not even

who you could be. And how could it be
that in such a place you would feel

more at home than at home,
at home in a place that you know

will never
inspire you

to be known,
where you'll always be that man, over there,

reading, a German perhaps, a Swede, nothing more
than a clue of clothes, a way of shaving, alone

in a public place
where you can be to yourself exactly

who you are,
but never more,

a viewer suspected, but never seen
on the other side of the screen?

How could it be that freedom is so
sweet and incomplete? ■

No Nets

for Rini

Mighty girl, standing in midair,
     one foot on a rock, the other
         on the crook of a wavery tree,
she is worriless
     as a supernatural being
         straddling the sky,
safe for a moment
in her father's gaze,
     his camera
     giving back to her
         his pride
         in who
         she's always been
            so she could see
        the proof
          when she needs it most,
             high wiring over sorrow
             and aching fright,
    without a doubt,
    never wavering, always
        the fearless
        explorer
        of her own delight. ■

Where We Are

for Rini

Wild Goose Island
with its four trees and brush and pail full of soil
piled in the middle of Lake St. Mary: a place
to dream a life that is
the dream of my life with you, where I
imagine myself as I am
living with you as you are, the whole
spacious
joy of it, of being
anonymous with you, just us
in a place just small enough,
just far enough,
just hard enough to get to
that it's always
just not there
for anyone but us. ■

Avebury Stones and West Kennet Long Barrow

Wheatfield wave
    rolling up out of the valley
        where bodies of stone
            circle the night,
      light carving through them
  like wind rivers streaming
            through green wheat seas
    as we move up and over
      the curling ground
to a crypt of stone in a barrow,
    a breaker of earth as old
      as the first dream of sailing,
    and sense in our souls
      that there's nothing to getting lost
    that moving can't fix:
    the great past,
      which never moves,
      never stays the same,
    rolls and plunges through our lives
      as fearless of death
      and losing its bones
as infinite seas
alive in the dreams of stone. ◼

from *Before Breakfast*

Power Preys on Privacy

Telling the whole
        truth about yourself
                violates
                a self-
                        confidence,
breaks the code
        of honorably savvy,
                self-interested
                        mistrust of all implications,
however refined, that privacies are
                                heresies
        too heavy for souls to mind
                as they should.
                Being undisclosed is made
                        unbearable because
                                we're told it implies
                        deep loneliness, which is
                                an exquisite social crime.
        Hermes, the farrier, god
                of truth bending, however,
        never lies.
        He offers up
                honest enigmas
                        not self-mutilations
                that garble the code:
                        like hanging your anger
                                by your own neck
                        so someone
                                you think is oppressing you now,
                will find you
                and suffer
                        more truth than you know. ■

The Liberty of Limitations

They were sawing him up.
He'd killed a prince.
And the punishment then,
in 1905, was to be
slowly deprived of your body
while still alive,
cut by cut,
too high on opium
to die or faint
but conscious of being
butchered
calmly before an attentive crowd.
I saw a photo of this in a book.
I saw the functionaries
in their Chinese caps
dutifully being as cruel as they could.
I saw his partially vanished body,
the acid white
silence
of his eyes.

I could bear but a glance;
I could not swallow it
anymore than I could swallow a fork.
So I closed the book and left him there
eighty-five years ago.
I did not have to know
the smoky black hollow of his face.
I could not
take him in,
I could not, and so
my life refused to let me try.
Like drowning fifty feet down,
it was all I could do.
I closed the book;
I removed my nerves from his body,
saved them for someone else, and left,
barely able to cross the street
but free to be
unable to do
who and what I am not. ■

Around the Next Corner

He turned up the street
and with the ease of buying a paper
saw the tanks,
saw one ram down the door
of a national register bank
and crush the chest of a vendor.
He saw flamethrowers gush through a mall,
napalming Penneys,
the hosiery, purses, and fake silk ties
geysering flame like fat on the stove.
He saw a man in line at the movies
pulled off by government punks
and heard his screams while he paid for two
tickets to darkness and pale escape
and then felt
the bayonet stab
through his own cheek,
the boot crack his spine,
and heard in his head,
like an ode to life,
the muse of truth
sing his escape
" . . . it really doesn't matter at all,
matter at all, matter at all. . . ." ■

Video Brain

One moment in Stalin's Russia
with Pasternak's Olga
locked in a white basement room
with tortured corpses,
staring in faces
looking for Boris's face,
learning too late
that she is the victim;
and the next moment
on Cumberland Street
in Marianne Moore's living room
with its neoclassical couches,
drop-crystal bouquets, toy tigers,
a clean butter dish in the fridge,
—her and her steeplejacks, Dodgers, four quartz clocks,
her "unaccommodating man,"
and that Southern, rubber band of voice—my hero.

Later that night, in my cave of books,
I believed myself the child of a modest fate,
while in Cambodia
farmers noticed with horror
their hands disappear in geysers of water,
blown off by blue, Chinese, anti-personnel mines
floating below the surface, around the rice
like Mara's lily pads,
planted by true believers who know
with all sincere and sweet conviction
they are doing the right
and useful thing.

It's all happening all at once.

How can I keep my innocence
from running out on the floor?

Think of Miss Moore more often.

She didn't waste who she was
fearing who she was not. She praised.

Remember her.
Try to be hopelessly wise.
Make your very small life much bigger
and forgive.

Praise is the poet's job.

But to praise
you must know,
and to know
you must feel,
and to feel
you must be
the child
of everyone's fate.

To praise,
you must forgive. ■

Death Row, Texas

for Leonel Herrera,
*executed by lethal injection, summer 1993**

Life is precious.
Your life is not.

Your life is less
important
than clearing the books,
    than never letting
    the conveyor belt stop,
    than a Justice's whim
        to tilt the last mile
        to a slippery slope,
            to make it a chute
            you can clean with a hose,
                with last meals sucked
                through tubes at a trot,
    to make it so all
    the accused
    are pre-hooded,
    pre-noosed, pre-IVed
            for The Drop
            through The Shutter
            of Now
            and Not.

New evidence doesn't matter;
the deadline means you're dead;
eyewitnesses,
    stolen from you by the state,
don't count,

if blind
    Justice can see
    you're just not there;
your kind's
too invisible
for your own good.

So your brown body
is velcroed down,
     dead weight on a gurney,
        your face replaced
        by a bar code of rules
   your mind,
        zipped up in a body bag
        long before your body,
   knowing for sure
   what no one else can:
that the Justice of the Universe,
      the Justice of Truth
            all dolled up in the Red, White, and Blue,
   is a false proposition,
      is Power's eternal bait and switch,
           its happy face, sucker punch, insider deal,
           its Big,
           shitty little
           Lie. ■

---

*Leonel Herrera was executed after the Supreme Court rejected his contention in Herrera v. Collins that a thirty-day limit under Texas law for seeking a new trial in capital cases is unconstitutional. Compelling evidence was presented ten years after his conviction that Herrera's deceased brother had committed the crime for which Herrera was sentenced to death. In a 6 to 3 decision, Chief Justice William Rehnquist wrote the majority opinion with Justices Blackmun, Stevens and Souter dissenting. Several weeks later, Herrera was killed.

Dancing Alone on a Floor Slick with Blood

It's like the first
rot of milk on the tongue
when you see
    that how they say it is
    and the way it is
are not the same;

when the boy
that you are
sees through
the trick that turns
    ideals
    into truths
    that are
    not real,
truths "more true"
than what actually happens:
    that war, let's say, is about
    clean shaven young men
    and not young men with their faces
        melting on fire.

What desolation
to see this when no one else does,
when you've lived your whole life
being told it's all OK
as they're cooing and feeding and patting your cares away.

For you, there's no way to know
why they say what they say;

they leave little clues
with no explanation,
slivers of glass
in the marshmallow Jello.
    Why
    would they leave it all up to you?

Inside the adorable bungalow
with lemonade and Grammy,
    with kitchen smells, pressed napkins, flowered plates,
    platters of buns and burgers,
    the swish of skirts
    the smell of pipes and martinis,
I peeked
at the evident,
page after page, all through
Life Magazine's
Illustrated Horror
of World War II:
    the incinerated face of a Japanese soldier
    and its silly "Hey, that's-death" grin;
    the beheading
    of a nice GI boy
        under a coconut palm;
    the Kamikazes and their distant eyes;
    the Jews,
        who looked just like me
        and the cooks in the kitchen,
    herded through streets
    like moths scooped up
    from a window ledge and washed
    with dusty iridescence down the drain.

Is this insane?

"Look, look at this,
come here, come here."
        "What?"
"Look at this."
        "Oh, that."
"Look!"
        "I've seen it."
"But look. . . ."
        "Come on, come on, let's go . . ."

Distractions never work for me.
I smelled the barbecue smoke
        and heard the luscious sizzle of the meat,
the only one who could see
        through the cellophane of the normal
where the flamethrower was
crouched behind the playhouse
        ready to exterminate
        the wrong insects
        with friendly fire. ■

middle

poems

1994–1978

from *Seven Deadly Sins: A Modern Psychomachia*

Pride

It becomes your soul: that sucking, itch, that mortal titter, blushing
under all the layers of your life, it knows you—that you're not
good enough for yourself. And so, the Oz contraption,

the trick transparency, the only out: to impress yourself, on others,
with yourself. It's done inside with props, with mirror mind pools,
two-way sylvan, with a funhouse warp, in which to gaze—triumphant,

the glory in your eye, presuming all the world is eager
for every nuance you contrive. But impressive others won't impress;
they're there inside, behind the mirror, peeping out at little you

buffooning, seeing nothing of the image of yourself you see,
only posturing and mediocrity. You know their eyes:
even you can see that who you are humiliates who you want to be,

that in comparisons like these, there's nothing left of you
but ironies, but pretensions at self-love which are self-mockeries.

Greed

It's not the having, or the hoarding,
it's a categorical thing, an abhorrence of less—it's the wanting,
wanting it all, wanting it all so much

you ceased to care for that part of the all that you already have,
and yet it's the very same thing that you're wanting, and so
both in the end are worth nothing at all. The absence is all

—don't settle for anything less, just ultimates
and ultimatums—like losing your life in haze of regret
for what it is not, demanding the absolute way it should be,

throwing away the wind, let's say, because it's at home
and not at sea, wasting good days, depressed,
possessed by the best they could be—wanting it all,

ignoring the stars you've charted for years
simply because they aren't all the rest.

Anger

A hard spot in the brain, a foetal core, it feeds
upon submission, swells, gets sore, a strangling pressure
that has to be appeased—and it is so easy to give in, so

helplessly fulfilling, it justifies all superstition:
No matter how brief or just, just to feel it, the bloating
of its hard sharp heat, the burning sweetness, is to know

the pleasure of an agony that is the opposite of love.
A mad opacity, it seals us in, makes us godly to ourselves,
permitting us to see only our own reality, to feel no cruelty

in our hardness, only violent right. Possessed
by this demon of our lives, our Hyde, a toxic constipation
forcing its relief, we sacrifice our lives, let go, enjoy it,

the elation of release; its birth: a poisonous self-titillation
in which our being is replaced by its own elimination.

Lust

Victims and idolaters, vacancies to solve, we pursue
such teasing expectations—not to be confused with excess, sex,
passions, and desires, but those mock familiar forms, icons

to appease us—seeing all we are, and must become,
completed for a moment in some likeness, some beauty, wanting,
peace or lie, external, statuesque, but belonging to our lives.

Embellishing extinction, cannibals, we specialize in bits and pieces
wooed from other lives, savoring deep semblances, charmed carrion,
irresistibly dismembered. Monsters, thus assembled, for us the crime is not

the wanting, but the harm—injustice—the used result: excluding them,
and all they are, for the worshiped parts we take from them,
giving our whole lives away at times for what we think will solve us,

make us whole, absolve us, charm us into idols, answers, bits and pieces,
lovers, prey for the teasing needs and vacancies of others.

Envy

Boas entwined, constricted, rigid in a single egg,
envy and lust are in the same bind: both make others
the final solution; but envy's the one that mangles with laughter,

the silliest sin, a total self-trade-in for somebody else,
a brain transplant for the good of the taker.
Ah, there he goes, the have-it-all hero, the donor you'd have

make you a victim. This host of your wishes: you'd scoop out your life
—utterly squander all that you are—to make room for the idol
you've made out of his. This is something much worse

than a groveling self-nihilation. By wanting to be who you are not
you toy with the tyrant's art—presuming that others are not
irreplaceable wholes, exclusively true to their beings, but

mere totals of stuff, sums with no soul or order, you render them down
to their easiest parts, so all the parts fit all the parts.

Gluttony

Like a thing that we know but won't understand,
we feel, one day, with the edge of our minds, a cannibal softness
take over the spine; tendrilling out like syrupy vines,

weaving, caressing, out of control, ravenous comforts
splurge through the bone, claiming the host the spine calls home.
And we find, one day, that we won't say no.

The parasite owns us, we do what it does: we indulge
luxurious "rights" and reflexes, growing immense,
inescapably soft, excreting a sweetness that covers the globe.

And then to our horror we know: we've become our own host,
lured by our own verdant decay—we cannot resist even this—
and sink, agape, capsized, euphoric, the sole superfluous

link in the chain. And the earth absorbs all that we've been
till all that is left is an interesting stain.

Sloth

Itching, soft, becalmed, asleep like snails
skidding in their shells, postponing our lives until the "right time,"
we go easy on ourselves, do nothing once again, say yes

over and over again, desperately at ease. Our energy ingrown,
self-poisoned, we watch in creamy horror as we bloat and hiss,
happy and appalled at the tepid lulling muck, the tempo of our wills,

on which we float, as our fate curls up from lack of use.
We know what we should do, do justice to our lives at least,
compete with chance, add choice to our sum of history and luck.

We know! But we can't, we can't start up. Misers,
paralyzed by habit, we arrive at the end too late for our lives,
full up and empty at the same time; the best of ourselves, our only duty,

put off each day, stillborn, without a breath—a gravid nullity
swelling with our time, creating, with our lives, a death. ■

from *Chaco Trilogy*

Chaco Body

I. Transparency

To imagine is to know
with no reference to the truth,
the truth which is without us
only pure.

We believe and we become.

Canyons, kivas, minds,
each contain a space
which is
what has contained it.

Power is in opening
so holy nothing is the way.

The canyon comes to you at dawn,
     as a god comes,
      full of prophecy, funereal,
light as gravity with nothing left to pull,
     as the past
     fills you
     as a void would,
                 exploding in
     as sun fills an open eye.

Here one wears the place as one would wear a mask,
is asked to join a dance one does not understand,
and does it,
        knows it,
        is it and is not,
in union
        with both doubt and play,
        and what one makes of doing.

There is no letter of the land,
no gospel code.
The literal means no more that what has formed it
as an instant means no more than what's behind, ahead.
The place is
everything it is,
in time, in mind,
its emptiness
and the front side of its stories.

Chaco body,
        deep breathing breezes through the weeds,
        rock face changing faces,
           imagination knows
           the present as transparency,
                deep vanishing,
                its mask of instants,
        knows
        what is
        is constantly not there,
        a focusing
        emerged into itself,
        over and over,
        layer by layer,
        a black hole, looking glass
        which holds it all,

its molecular days,
its oceans, corpses, gods,
its depths and surfaces of light,
the weight
of its transparencies, stratigraphies,
its harmonies of scree clack,
clouds of river foam, their floating by,
shorelines lapping,
sharks cruising through the cliffs,
flood gusts, virga, lightning far as dreams,
and water in the ditches,
the sound of bells, of beaks, of rattle flutter,
the wondering
in living skulls
in spirit face
risen from the light beneath
to stand
in moon air,
hearing still
vibrations
from other worlds, heart drums
in the round soundings of the night
deep underground
where souls diffuse into their flesh
and imagination waits
as possibility in nerves.

Transfigured here,
to imagine is to wear
the mask of endless once,
the canyon
            uttered on your breath
into the space that covers you
as emptiness is covered, instant by instant,

as dreaming
       hardens into sense
so you can vacate where you are,
filled as a mask is filled
with being that is neither
form nor soul
but possibility
worn inside
so you can play at being where you are,
remote, remorseless,
dancing away, unchanging,
circular, in upheaval, straight ahead.

It is dead,
where future dies,
and all around you
you inside
transparent as the lens of now.
And somewhere in the seeing
you disappear,
mind becomes its space,
and your eyes themselves
are openings in time.

II. Already Gone

Never freed from now,
I cannot hear them,
      I can have
                        no memory of their lives.
                        Their voices are behind me
      even though I am
          what they have left behind.

As if time
were whole
and still behind the lives of those
who cannot hear me now,
                  I am the heir
    of their imagining,
                       and am,
                       myself,
                       no more
                       than what
  cannot be known tomorrow.

In the human now
we know them as ourselves.

It was so
on the walk to La Fajada in the polished heat,
the sun inhaling, holding its breath;
it was so
        when nine
        hundred years
        across the dead sand, scrub, and ants
a clump of grasses whirled and hissed
so violently I felt
the holy panic in myself,
the terror vacancy, adrenal gorging and the dread
to hear
        what must have been
        the passing of a god
        with no one left there
                    to believe it.

Believe the fossil fin,
the tide pool ripples on the canyon wall.
Believe divinity filling voids.

Our questions are the same,
formed from stories
    we cannot know,

                stranded in our nows.

    But I say,
    as I read the day,
    that the land has memory,

                    that the past must
              come to it,
              that it is
      unconsciousness itself,
that there
we all
    are visitors without guides
              in the un-
              recollected memory
        of the world.

We are the heirs of all imagining.

Because the canyon knows the death I am,
I know myself
as carapace,
      as lightning freed,
      long gone in light,
    as myth again
    which is to truth
           as bodies are to death,
                mortal as rock,
           as dreams passing through rock,

                        alive
        with dying,

                    present
                    by being unrecalled,
                a fine silt
                waiting for wind,
                                        true
                                        as a god
believed through the grasses.

III. Balancing Zero

Breathing in,
                one pays attention
as waterdrops
with nuclei of dust
                        add up
to mud clouds piling
                            geographies of breath
                            too great
                            to think across,
inaccessible to feet.

Breathing in,
one pays attention to the day
in rain pools
                    upside down,
            the sky
on the surface of the water,
water on the surface of quiet mud,
motion
on the perfectness of light.

Breathing out,
one pays attention to the distances of myth
too great to think across:
                              the canyon floor
a map of matter's inwardness,
a truth so distant
we can only see
                    the edge light of its skin
as we handily traverse it
in our bodies
                after lunch.

Breathing out,
one pays attention to the slowness all around,
to change we know but cannot find,
to landscape symbols
static as the past,
and dead,
              though overhead
        cloudlands go
                before our eyes,
                  if we look away,
air mud moving
as the land we look from moves.

Breathing,
one pays attention
to the edges
                    of the air,
                    of the eyes that see the air,
              of the brain that knows the edges
              as they fold and open on
              the edges of our lives;
one pays attention
to the lungs,

to what one thinks of mind,
                    of inside horizons
where being has no edges
and the self exchanges with the canyon
all itself
            —the place itself
            as intimate and distant as the brain,
edgeless
to the blood that feeds it
with the air around the mind
and on the surface of our sight,
edgeless to the light of suns
as to the light of nerves
lightning with each word.

IV. Traces

 . . . mind bones . . .
carcass stones
                    of how ideas
                                    shape themselves through matter
. . .
Dreams of permanence!
" . . . age under-ate them."
                        Rock skin,
human bark
built up by lives
                longing for a cadenced breath
 . . . and order . . .
                    wall face
                        shoring time
                        by imitation,
                                    damming change
                        with canyon shape,
                                        eroding

with raw being
                    the ocean of cacophony
          before the rhythm seen by myth:
                    Muscle makes it music,
                    the patterning of days
                    laid down
                    by hands,
                              stone by stone . . .

Imagination forms the land
into a body for the soul,
armor for the flesh,
a mental nest,
                    skull house,
                    safe,
                              so mind
                              thrives
within a world that it is not, can
come home to it,
                    can make it seem
as if the world could shape itself
into a human form,
                    a formal friendliness,
                    natural as ideas.

Sunlight shines in only ruined rooms.

. . . roof earth,
cedar shag,
pebbled topsoil overhead . . .

Moonlight in your eyes inside
is as dawnlight
washing over corpses
caverned by decay.

    Yet in this
                     anatomy
we see stratigraphy
          of masonry,
                  not Venuses in stone,
but layering as beautiful
as the body of the rock
. . . an icon,
             kachina
                 of geography,
of the power
of the land
             which people can transform
             because the land
                will
give itself
to people who are not apart.

. . . ruins now,
spine stone disks exposed
where columns once upheld
the kiva roof weave's
yantra round of trees and weeds
                        . . . room hoards hollow,
roof beams now
holes in stone,
like families are,
and clans and god form are,
                  squared spaces,
circles,
        in the slowest dancing of the rock.

Bonito, Alto, Chetro Ketl
—not artifacts alone,
             not Parthenons

but myth shapes of a union
they did not deny.

. . . these bodies of our images.

Imagination bonds
the future,
            past and perfect,
                where to journey is a trial
of recollection
        as we know
                 that even we
are ruins
of some wholeness
            . . . shadows, traces
of relationship,
of fuller harmonies,
potentials,
      beautiful
        in our mortality
as ruins,
        and,
as everything that is
without perfection,
           perfect as it is.

V. Like a Rock

Imagination is the land.

. . . muse of water,
  muse of stone,
of holiness that's clothed
in sand and weather,

in presence
as it comes to us

                across the mind

to convince us
of realities
more than merely real.

Nightland lifting,

              the canyon
              filling up with light

as minds fill
and fall away,

        fragile
      as the history
of how the grasses move,
blade by blade, second by second.

Intimate land:

           The canyon

is a silence
in the center of a Self
weightless as the silence of the rock,
a silence that is felt

      pretending you're not there,
      sitting still with stones
    to be weathered by the day,

                  forgetting
who you are,

      lost like friends, dead sins,
      like breath

           that rock time won't contain,

a stone eye opened
as eddies of birds
blow past

      worlds within worlds.

              Behind your sight:

the blackness of the molecules,
topographies of faith,
                    distance
dense as stone,
                motionless,
                dangerous with grace,
the silent breathing
of the God of Gods
whose name
        nobody knows. ■

Chaco Elegies

I. The Same Sweet Folly

There are those to whom we are vermin,
or sources of food, or impediments
along the way
to the "inevitable."
There are days when the sky tries to blow us away,
or drown us or dry us up
and we resist.
We hold in common
this Resistance
to change that discounts us,
holding onto our doors
like ants against other ants
holding on
against trifling horrors,
holding on
to our gardens
our children,
our calm nights,
all of us in Troy,
in Argos, Cuzco,
in Chaco and Hopi,
in Watts, Los Chavez, and East LA,
this family of the homely
clinging to home.
Time is no barrier between us.
We are continuous as the history of air.
In the Resistance
we learn
to want nothing
to be
less important
than us,

to diminish
only   ·
the demon
jerking the hand of the grabber.

II. Time's Common Sense

Change
is divine
exercise,
       Her practice,
       Her meditation.
Returning
to an again
which is always
a never,
       I know
       we have looked at the clouds together,
       looked at the stone together,
       have breathed in the night together
      —all of us who have known
       the canyon as ourselves.

At Chaco I know I am not alone.
I know I have heard even Homer
weaving the tides of his stories,
and Sappho singing lullabies alone in the night,
heard the footdrums in Rinconada
like ancient surf through the stone.
This is the place
where the past remains.
Utterly changed,
        the landscape
        is the same.

The future happens so fast,
it's too fast to dread.
And now
the future is as good
as already over again.

That is the teaching of the land,
its way of life,
a way to be with time,
to become time.
It is all we can know of Her,
and a practice to become Her,
a Great North Road, a birth canal,
a way to be born
to life and death
and home again.

Where I stand
they stood;
my body is theirs,
as my body is the boy I was,
as the canyon is the place it was,
new cells,
new life,
new being every moment,
always,
always,
never ending.

III. Mother of Myths

We read of the Hopi (that's all we can do)
that the dead are clouds,
that the dead rain down their souls on earth,
that life depends on their essence.

I felt a closing when my mother died,
felt the past had pulled itself from my life;
where she was
now was nothing.

Where did she go?

Is she anywhere more than a sorrow,
more than something gone?

I am starving for new stories.

I have no heaven for her, no Elysium.
She isn't waiting, in pillows and poppies,
for curtain calls from the gods.

She is a memory
        I often forget
        has no memory itself.

But at Hopi
the dead never leave.
Rain is soul.
And the souls of Chaco
still feed them.
All history's in the sky,
the crops, their bodies.

Any meal is a communion.

But my mother and I are as far apart
as I am from faith
in the Fall from grace.

She is like the canyon was on a Tuesday
seven thousand years ago, or a Monday just last month,

a detail
in the history of time.

The canyon is
every day it was,
as the species is
every person it has been.

But she
    is my mother,
    not a day in the shape of stone,
    and I don't know where she is.

She is not in her bones,
not in her ashes I put in the waves.

She is an idea
I have not yet formed
like clouds unborn in the sea.

I want her home with me. I want
    death, all death, to be
    a right proximity.

In Chaco, at least, I know
the canyon is
where the past remains.

I know it is not
    only now.

So *can* I say
it is time's common grave,
a mother of myths,
where death conceives, where memory
gives birth to the future?

Can I say she is somewhere there
waiting for doubt to leave?

IV. Trusting Blindness

It is always night there.
The holy darkness still exists
without a light to tease us,
teaching us to see
                        with our eyes
                            closed,
trusting blindness with our hearts
                                    as night world visions,
                                    erasing the profane,
                                    replace right now with myth
                                    where time is all at once
the "mountain around
which all moving is done."
                            now and forever
                                    without sense,
                                    like us,
blind in the truth of hope all-knowing.

It is always night there
and I am not afraid of the dark,
crossing a spine of stone into Walpi,
a guest following guides
                            into the holy past
                            from the holy present,
                            hoping for new sight,
disappearing into a cloud of snow
                                    and reappearing
                                        at 2:00 a.m.
on the other side of the mind
                            to feel

imagination dance,
blind to reason,
where we,
brittle with fright,
abandon fear,
like children can,
to trust
in human good
to see us through a universe
we'll never understand,
a universe unknowable except
for masks and faith
met at night
when all gods walk
the wine dark streets
like pilgrims through mountains of the sea.
And right now is
all nows,
so close
we feel it
all in our breathing,
in the graying woman
keeping time against her hand
with the braid of the girl she is rocking
in the kiva's grace,
right now
suspended
across ten thousand nights,
a full moon frozen,
lighting holy forms
surging from the dark
to give us candy:
our delight
their faith

as they dance away
>   though the All
>   Possible Source
>   of now, of all
that was, and all
that never was,
where it is always night,
darker than the middle of the brain,
where no one can see
>   but only trust
that faith
in goodness
>   is a kind of sight.

V. Joy with No Difference

Practicing the canyon,
I feel my emptiness
forget me
>   for a moment longer than it takes
>   to change and stay the same.
Practicing to be
the willingness of stone,
the bodylife of ravens
loafing on the clouds,
practicing the canyon,
>   I can see
>   how life and death
>   have no difference to speak of,
>   like one second from the next.

Practicing like this
nothing matters more
than anything,
for all things are
empty as forgetfulness

is full
of its unknowns,
like time is
everything it's been in you, so full
you are
everything
that didn't happen, too.
                                        Practicing and practicing,
you might become the space
                                                        and the form around it,
all that's there
and all that's not—
                                        the shape of your mind
                                        the canyon's shape;
you might fit with it
as bodies fit,
                                as light fits with shadow,
                                as faith, itself, might fit with truth
                                as fate fits with fact. ■

Chaco Mind

I. Garden Music

On the graves of gardens
in Chaco's inner shore,
      I hear the music of time,
spanning the holy once
from the end to the beginning.

Here I am allowed to know
      the other side
      of mythlessness
behind the empty voices, pageless books,
the blank mask of fact, and all
      our boring horrors,
      purposeless but for gain,
and the snotty
      kisses of power.

On the graves of gardens
      beneath the face of the deep,
I see the other side
      in the mirror of my mind,
      as on the surface of the vanished sea
  .   or in my own free garden
where the present is
      as it was before
when persons, beasts, plants, the planet, and the gods
      all shared alive
the same living place.

On the graves of gardens
      in Chaco's tidal soul,

I know that now
    is the garden long ago
that always soon will be.
    Here in the presence of the stone,
witness to all the storms,
    memories of the future
allow me to recall
    one canyon morning a thousand years ago
when the first, adored, bright infant green
    surfaced through the bony rubble.

Who saw it first that year,
    bursting up
    through flakes and grit,
    up into the deep sea gray of the dawn
    where I stand now
    in oceans of holy corn
        I remember like ideas
    I've just forgotten?

  Am I the child
    who saw it first that spring?
(The front
    and the back
    are part
    of the same.)

On the graves of gardens
    in Chaco's testing grace,
I know the other side
    is now
in truth I cannot say,
    truth I only know
because I trust
    my animal sense of it.

Here in the canyon,
even stone knows
what numbers cannot tell,
even wind knows
what fact denies.
  Here on the graves of gardens
I see myself
at the moment that I die,
dreaming truth about the other side:
     that I'm alive,
     right now,
in gardens
   my dreams
will treat one day
      as holy.

II. The Music of Time

It is all one sea,
one sky,
  to the edge
  of the end.

At Pacific's rim off Malibu,
  sailboats slicing through a sunny fog,
we watched the waters
swallow Chaco up,
and we could see
  no difference
on the surface of the sea.

And as the waves changed places,
the sea between us
was made of ashes

and the air of days,
        days like drops of rain,
like mist, so many days
one after another
       endless
       without beginning.

      (There is
         nothing
   more.
         There is
         nothing
         other.)

On Chaco days
     when shirts are sails,
  and wind works dust like water,
I've seen sharks' teeth, like weeds,
cropping up on sandstone flats, have held in my hand
a slab of fish, rock fins and scales flat as shale.
I've seen the nacre of shells, like angel skin
budding through the surface of the rock.

Before "death
and its questionable past,"
I understood so little.
I thought I put my mother's ashes in Pacific Seas,
     released her to the waves
     and she was gone.

But now, the ocean's sound
is just her breathing,
my mind rising and falling
     with the tide of days
   on Chaco's inner shore;

my father's ashes
and my own with hers
rising up in thunderheads
        chasing poets off the cliffs
        with lightning fact
that burns through words
so faith, for once,
        is purified of form.

As ghost clouds
boil across the stone flats
with eons of the moon,
I feel her like a thought
released without a sound,
        and see
no difference
on the surface of the sea.

III. The Cave of Generation

We know the past is fiction,
now does not exist,
the future cannot be
till nothing's left of it.
        We know this
and we don't
know more or less
what we know.
      We sense
          the paradox
          of then,
that flux of tense
      —the almost now
     and the lost ago—

those atoms
in the weight of self,
that flood the skull,
       the theater
       of our stories,
that cave of time
upon which all
identity depends.

We cannot be without our stories.
Even if we know them to be false
                 as dreams are real,
they are
where we take place,
       until the mythless
       twists them into "truths"
demanding faith
in the false-
    face of acts
    molded clearly over motives
    that falsify the faith,
               and we retreat
betrayed
to the cave, the paradox of then,
where first things happen
      and wait
      for generation
      free of force.

We know the mythless world
erases stories
like fanatics reform cultures
by chopping off a million heads.

But caves are not ways out;
they are ways back,
as all beginnings are returns.

> (Now is
> a holy
> place.)

Despite the loss
of all the images of our trust,
some of us each time
take the dark walk
through the cave of the mind
                    and return

                              as the persons
                              we would become,
slowly
broken to the truth,
              by doing
utterly no more
than what we choose
naturally
to do each day.
                    When I return
I arrive at Bonito's
rounded back of perfect bone
the cave of generation,
and feel my attention open
to what I find,
              waiting
for what appears
pure of motive
                    as the stone,
                    irresistible
as what has happened
just before
              it happens.

IV. Waiting for Shooting Stars

for Rini, Jim, Jacki, Marc, Chris, John, Francis, and Ian

I have never physically been to the top,
star waiting on La Fajada Butte.
But I would not need to be told
how to be
      if they, long ago,
        should find me there in their minds,
a useless dream shape
from who knows where.
            I know enough.

      (The sacred
               and profane
               are sacred.)

I know that hills and peaks
are the cores
of caves and the deep;
that everything fits;
that the present
is the core of the past—
        so I know
        what is there
        at the top
as a novice knows
what is to be known
in places too holy
for knowing alone.

We go to a hill each New Year's Eve,
and watch the sky on our backs among shards,
backed up to rabbit grass knolls,
waiting for shooting stars.

We are children in this,
knowing the truth
without
being it yet.

And I remember there
        the old watchers on La Fajada
waiting and waiting,
working not to wait,
working not to want
                something to happen.

On my back on the hill
        I know I know nothing,
will never know anything else
                but what I can guess:
that the dream dark sea of space and time
is real
        beyond thought,
that we witness
the edge of a fact vaster than death ever was,
that the whole
        endless
        enterprise of the atoms
results in love
as real as the stars ever are.

I need nothing more.
Stars give light;
            I see it.
Humans love;
            I feel it.
Proof enough.

In the wild, serene,
      annihilating
      night,
             we are real,

    we belong.

    We are real.

V. Running to Wijiji

When you know who you are
you do who you are,
polishing a mountain
        without a goal.

      (There is
      nothing
      more.
      There is
      nothing
      other.)

At ten,
I did who I was;
I had no choice;
      knowing and doing were not apart;
and where I was
was as much of myself
              as what I did.

(Now is
a holy
place.)

Then years of trying
    and coming apart,
polishing stones
not the mountain
until
  the canyon
  wore me away
so I could see myself
              singular as rocks,
       as shadows, clouds,
       as cliff curves, edges,
       water scars and swirls,
real as skin,
clear as sudden change,
      my body
           opening to the stars
      like Chacra Mesa
      on the skull of the world.
Now at fifty,
I am the place again.
      (The front
      and the back
      are part
      of the same.)

At ten, the place
     was a forest street
where I did who I was,
    biking to escape
  tender failures,
sailing through arbors of high ponderosas,
winding like grassy streams
            through Saturday morning sun.

When you are who you are
you do who you are.
        (The sacred
        and profane
        are sacred.)

At dawn near La Fajada,
breathing in
the rising light,
        I am
ten and fifty all at once.
Running through fossil fields of corn,
running the cool space of canyon shade
as one runs memories through the gorge of time,
I see myself
        in the shadow at my side,
bike rider, now
        dawn runner
reaching Wijiji
         at
         the
        moment
the sun
        blooms
wildflower light,
    lightning white
over the canyon rim,
over the edge of my brain.
        Stunned by God
  again and again,
            why should I doubt
      any longer?

Coda

Now is
a holy
place.

There is
nothing
more.
There is
nothing
other.

The front
and the back
are part
of the same.

The sacred
and profane
are sacred. ■

Geodes

And creatures fashioned wonderfully appear.
—Virgil, *Georgics*, Book IV

Forms, though a lifetime, arise
    from the mind's full life,
forms of meanings not wholly known,
    seeking in use,
their completion through time
    to inform the mind
of its own secrets.
    For you, with your lavish
official precision,
    competitive muse, for you, Virgil:
the disciplined land,
    its heraldic bees
so ordered they seem
    satires of state,
so willing they need
    not be humbled to serve
your Caesar messiah,
    tamer, reviver
of nature's state,
    your state of grace,
the Roman world hive and heaven.

For me, diffident, slow, obscured,
    for me the geode's become
the form that I use
    for what I'm not sure

I know how to say.
    Their hardnesses surround
vanished lives
    in limestone or in shale,
animals and plants that left their space
    for waters in the sediment to fill
and form chalcedony, hard foam,
    that cloud stone, roiling shell
of thunderheads, that hardens
    in the ground and cracks
to let new waters in that grow
    internal firmaments
inward through the void
    —these creature graves replaced
with water gems that spread
    as history spreads through brains
in soundless dark, orphic caves
    in which decay transfigures
into secret stone, as though
    fossils of holy lives in catacombs;
the universe itself
    hidden in the darkness that it fills.

The forms of meaning
    have meanings of their own.

Your bees, your Caesar, and your law
    —mastered nature your citizen's delight—
disguise, in weaves of discipline's conceit,
    the secret of human crime—
contained no less
    behind the kindest face—
that history refined

in Washington or Rome,
in Vulcan's Cave, Los Alamos,
     that rests in each of us, an art and fate,
waiting its release again
     in strategies, mob truths, machines, "steel harvests,"
in sanctions for the family men
     whose atrocities are security.

Within such hardnesses,
     poets open into art
another fate. Risking history,
     boredom, atrocity, denial,
it is their use
     to be a privacy for others,
a candidness through form,
     vanishing in art to leave
a shaping space for other minds to fill.
     And from such fullnesses
creatures fashioned wonderfully appear,
     species of meaning that live between minds,
proof in themselves of something more,
     of something hidden always
in our grief, hidden as tranquility,
     surprise, are hidden, as revelation is
in the acts and flesh shapes we are known by.
     And this is enough to sustain us,
even in Rome, in even
     the abscess deep, throbbing
world of the crumbling
     mushroom dome. ■

Hiding Out

It was right in the heart of the deadliest place,
the dead heart of it all,
right in the wires and scented grease,
the thrumming and error and speed;
even night in that place was too bright for your eyes
and hulking above the midsummer trees
the vicious pink facades,
masking those alien wasp-waisted towers,
seeping deformity, money, and death.
That's where it was, our triumph,
our invisible life
all wrapped up in its dollhouse wrapper.
We lived to pretend no one knew we were there.
There was always the chance, we knew;

all anyone had to do
was open the gate and come in,
but nobody did, until then.
So there we were, disguised in our lawn,
free from agreeing and needing to please,
secure in that sweet addiction of ours:
our fortress garden far from the street
—a miniature, model,
a distant view only we could inhabit, in which
the present itself was as good as the past
when it causes the smiles of desire.
The plan of it all was a labyrinth built
of cypress tree hedges trimmed to resemble high walls,
an impossible pattern of spiraling shade, filled

with alcoves and flowers, with bowers for reading,
arbors and vines, with tables for thinking, glass cases,
stores for the mind—this shrine to the Swiss
Family Robinson, Robinson Crusoe, this place
with its pantries and wicker divans,
its vegetables rising from bays of raked sand,
its aqueducts lined with wild agate.
There was always the chance,
it had to be—the world delights
in seams to pry open; it made us feel free,
neither safe nor exposed,
but snug and ferocious
with passageways every which way,
and always the tunnel through which to escape
to that chamber of fact down below,
that chapel we'd carved, so perfectly dark,
an effigy shape of our totem the shell, in the deepest
recesses of which we had placed
the inner reaches of snails cracked open—there
where their genes said they were safe—
displayed like the brainpans of martyrs.
Our cunning was thorough, and so precise,
we could even escape our seclusion.
Each night we would go
to the looking place circle, the center
of all our design, and empty our minds
into the sky, without leaving a trace behind.
Night in that place was too bright for your eyes,

so we'd close them and see
the inviolate view, the darkness inside us
flooded with stars
—our skulls and the sky
seamless crusts of cataract blue,
masking the cosmos in which we were lost,
secrets without any clues.
How happy we were. How silly.
Each day we would play
we were geodes of space, starheaded spies
burrowing through the pink facades, small irritations
in the mind's eye of the future upon us, sent as proof
its illusions were flawed, that it too

had seams to pry open, that
no matter how hard it tried
there would always be some
exception it could never quite find.
When I think of it now
it all seems so fast, so petty,
as if it had happened during a nap.
Our invisible life,
our triumph, the sky—when they found it,
they just pushed it in,
pulled everything out, put us off to one side,
weren't even rude,
drained it, swabbed it, sprayed it with grease,
then filled it for good with their numbered confetti. ■

Pretending Who I Am

I tell you, there is a space between myself.
It's where stutterers get stuck,
jammed between wrong words and meaning.

Actors know
they're not their own creation.
They are owned
by how we use them,
as I am owned.

It is best not to say too much,
just wear white suits and sit
in cool white chairs
and write long books
on a few white cards.

Stutterers know
performance
is contortion.

Oh the muscular face,
the twists and gapes,
the acrobatic smile.
We hate your gaze,
the mirror of your eyes
that diminishes our size,
makes perfect models of our lives.

It's not your fault.
You're just a test,
a range for me to see
how real I can be before you.
You'll never know.
When I am seen,
you give my likeness back to me.
But no one can feel
how it feels to miss,
how useless it feels to hit
in forests of misses too deep to approach,
how it feels to be on fire
—even we can't feel it
after it's through.
There is a space between me.
Hero, hunchback,
nice boy, Casanova
I want to talk stiletto,
razor speak,
speak to be heard,
to be heard as I think.
But I can hear the oracle
bend down and say,
"be not history,
be of use,
waste not
the body of truth,
risk not being
by seeming to be,
be not their fantasy
between who you are."

Contortionists perform no meaning.
Drool is not symbolic.
Tyrone Power, Vincent Price,
their masks are second nature
in your gaze.
I wanted one so, I stitched it on;
it was never, though, a graft.
Pretending how I am
is natural as lying;
it's just the truth.
Masks fill up with life
to match their features.

Quiet, quiet.

The truth is not embarrassing.
You grow
into the image and likeness
of yourself; your face
the front of what's behind it. ■

christmas

poems

2005–1969

Solstice

perfect
clear light
star mind
chorus
eye star
joyous
pulse light
clear
nerve star
pulse sight
heart bright
chorus
joyous joyous
all one
light

perfect
clear light
star mind
chorus
eye star
joyous
pulse light
clear
nerve star
pulse sight
heart bright
chorus

joyous joyous
all one
light

perfect
clear light
star mind
chorus
eye star
joyous
pulse light
clear
nerve star
pulse sight
heart bright
chorus
joyous joyous
all one
light ■

Oracle News

Christmas 2005

The Oracle wasn't
all washed up at all.
But hope
is a real tough calling.

She used to knit scarves
to make her points,
warm with bromides, formerly wise,
still true:

> *Know Thyself*
> *Moderation Wins*
> *You Must Change Your Life*
> *The Readiness Is All*

Few read them.
So she took to speaking
like so much graffiti:

> *God Is Home Sweet Home,*
> she scribbled on boxcars along the way.

Then she made up some Christmas weather
out of the words of any old poet who came along.
One, denser than most, she heard pleading,
How *do* I change my life?
Is it true you can make
small adjustments
and everything falls into place,

like curing a limp
by good posture alone.
Is that right?

> *Don't worry about what's right,*
> she scrawled on fence posts.
> *It will come to you as strange advice.*

It's not your fears
that matter, is it, the poet blurted,
not those over-excavated,
looted digs, the archaeology of our terrors,
    not the bird flu,
    the terrorists, and hurricanes,
    cancers, tortures, humiliations, ice caps
    melting, poison gas, white phosphorous,
    vanishing oil, soiled water, war,
    not the demons of insult and disregard,
    the horror gods of paranoia?

> *No. Why change?*, she sprayed on bridges.

What matters is doing good,
for goodness sake. Isn't it?,
the poet wrote on his hand with a ball-point pen.
Let's not be lured
by the dope
of posthumous glory,
your whole life reduced
to merely the sound of your name.

A joying we will go,
　　a joying we will go,
　　　　she painted on railroad ties in Laramie, Wyoming.

Think of the relief you feel
if you could just stop
the drip, drip, drip
of cavernous complaint,
the inner whine, the low-grade fever
of sweaty carping, the gobbling,
eternal, dead-end critique, ragged
like the buzz of sirens in your ears,
the bells of St. Tintinnus stilled.

　　Ho, ho, ho,
　　a joying we will go,
　　hi ho the happy o,
　　　　she scratched in fresh cement.

The oracle could feel her audience
turning away, straining to hear

the sweet, low wail of the damners,
and damned reformers and their giddy harps.

"How do I change my life?" the old poet pleaded.

Ho, ho, ho,
a joying we will go;

I told you so, I told you so,
a joying sweet and slow,
     she doodled in Missoula.

Is that it?,
the old poet scolded.
What about resentments,
cleaning them out
like blowing your nose
of night's debris,
that first release,
the oily dust of hurt,
incapacity, betrayal
sneezed up the chimney
with a "Happy Trails!"

     Is that you, Santa Claus?
     she penned on casts and braces all over the world.

     Think of the fondest
     dreams of ice.
     Now there's some strange advice,
     she quipped on the sands of Waikiki.

When ego is replaced,
when acquiescence is erased,
what is
works out
into what
will be,

without
using you
as manure,
the old poet doodled as if in a duel.

Dashing through the snow
knowing what you know,
hope is free to grow and grow
when it lets you go,
she scribbled on bags of cat food.

A joying we will go,
a joying we will go,
good's in sight
and life is right
there's nothing more to know,
she whispered into nurseries.

Rosa Parks,
now there's a hero.

Your mind's not to blame.
It wanders. Learn to ride it,
she iced on scones in Nova Scotia.

But why is mind:
mind what I say,
and I don't mind,
and never mind?

Paths exist, like mice trails
through the scrub and snow.

Don't find out what it's like
to be old without being wise.

Take the numinous where you find it,
she wrote on the soles of sneakers.

We can't be told,
but we know
that worry
has added
nothing
to nothing,
to nothing!

Be at home in happiness,
she jotted on the windshields of a billion cars.

Protect only
your openness.

Can you tell
joy from success,
freedom from rebellion,
happiness from getting what you want?,
she chalked over playgrounds.

What's bliss?
she wrote on the clouds.

The supreme,
sweet, kindness
of choice,
and the miracle
of the chance
that it matters.

Knowing nothing
is wrong
in world that is
what it is
what it is
what it is
what it is.

Take sides,
Choose joy,
the Oracle sighed across the windows of the world.

You must change your life.
Don't find out what it's like
to be old without being wise. ■

Five Rebellious Pleasures

Christmas 2002

I. Being Calm

It's such a trick to play on power,
seeing through the feeble madness of the news.
What a comforting rebellion to be calm,
to refuse to goose step with the nearest fool.

Calm never lets us forget
how fearlessness is sweeter
than the dearest freedom granted by another.
Only one thing works, and it

can't really be spoken, except to say
that love will not deplete us, that generosity
is an ease so steely true, it overrules
blank cruelty every time, unbounded,

free as the calmness of leaves
reclining to the snowy ground.

II. Knowing What We Really Think

We are told the world is falling apart,
that nothing will ever be the same.
Don't believe it till you see it.

Sometimes humor is the only test,
an acid jest. Let's go see for ourselves
if the joke's on us:

our own way of thinking spreads out before us;
we are the first to see its false horizons;
the first to report if the old maps are right,

or criminally charmed and wrong.
What a joke on force it is
to know our own minds. It makes us

like truth is, stronger than the strongest
and stronger than the worst.

III. Peace

In the early, distant, first freedoms of the morning,
when we're released of all reproach and all encroachment

we can feel the torture of old anger for what it is,
the silly death blows ego tried to give to conscience.

It used to feel so noble, that pain we couldn't bear.
But now, to live as if the whole world were asleep,

moving wide awake through its nightmares with a hush,
that's a peacefulness we cannot seek

in the way we try to understand why a strange day,
vaguely sad, isn't worth the sorrow when it's over.

What if we all woke up, free and early one morning
and lived the rest of our lives as if we were safe,

as if it had dawned on us
there's nothing left for us but trust.

IV. Kindness

It catches everyone off guard.
It's an affront to fear.
It pushes the absurd smothering of joy
back out the door.
What a sweet dissent to refrain
from brutal truth.
        Honesty for the sake of honor
has ruined everything it's touched.
Fulminate to yourself, but shut up for awhile.
Break the rules. We were made for acts of kindness.
All the rest—the suspicion, the nastiness, the greed—
is a bumbling, pitiful fraud,
        and even indelible time
just wants to forget it.

V. Forgetting

It's not stupid to be unafraid.
Mistakes do not replace us.
How happy it makes the stars

when we douse our pettiness and they can feel
all our tiny generosities
glow like interstellar dust.

Who's to say that such and such a wretchedness
makes a whole life sour? What a final act
of defiance it would be

to forget the pain, the wrong, the shame, the panic,
and know with "certainty and praise"
that love does not deplete us, that the beauty

of whole lives can be seen sometimes
if we only look the other way. ■

Five Least Fallible Pleasures

Christmas 2001

> *Pleasure is not an infallible critical guide,*
> *but it is the least fallible.*
> —W. H. Auden

I. This Is No Time to Be Vague

Purpose is a pleasure, the sly sage smiled.
This is no time to be vague. The whirlwind consumes
even the hands of the infants. We can't wait
for pain to get out of the way. Our whole world aches.
An old man screams, "What does peace mean?
I'm afraid of losing my self-respect."
There's no safe time to know your mind.
What's the purpose in waiting for truth
and hearing a voice, too late, late at night,
say "I inwardly did nothing,
O Iscariot-like crime."*

What is the purpose? What do you mean?
Let's clean our minds and know what we know.
Kindness is a truth always worth trying.

II. Otherwise Can't Be

Sense is out of the question.
We're hated, we're loved
—no matter the explanation.

---

*From Marianne Moore's "In Distrust of Merits"

This happened, that didn't. That's it.
Nothing can be otherwise.
Acceptance is not resignation.
What sweet pleasure, then,
when resentment stops bawling.
What *does* peace mean?, the dying child will ask.
We can always pretend
we're effective,
though "certainly the means
must not defeat the end."*
Finally, we must answer.
Another question just won't do.
We will try "kindness," and try
being kind, and we'll think
it's not enough, somehow.
But the child will know.

III. "Hunt-Mad Hubert Startled into a Saint"†

It doesn't take much.
Vile catastrophe is more than enough
to shock us back to dangerous living.
Who doesn't, in her deepest heart,
want to help with all she has?
There is a best and worst.
Conduct measures it.
The best overwhelms us every time
a person opens to another's need,
or yields in strength.

---

*From Marianne Moore's poem "Values in Use."
† From Marianne Moore's poem "Saint Nicholas."

The best is there in the soft night of the mind,
when we feel with all we know that nothing can
go wrong, or is wrong, or ever will be wrong. And yet
the worst won't disappear.
The old woman pleads through her tears,
"What does peace mean?"
Her heart, filled up with the question,
is so patiently free, the truth
just baffles us with its secret joys.

IV. Innocent Merriment

A whole biology of beautiful smiles,
winters calm as ravens shadowing through the pines;
dancing on cyclones we say
the bottomland truth to each other,
and Santa Claus finds his way to your beautiful heart
in the dark of the Christmas light parade.
We sleep the sleep of the blest
on the rim of the steepest decay.
"It's a pleasure to see so
much confusion."*
Merrily, merrily, merrily, merrily,
life is such a dream.
"What does peace mean?" he whispered,
remembering a hand on his wrist long ago
so warm, so deeply kind, he minds nothing anymore
of the crumbling life he leads.

---

*From Marianne Moore's poem "The Steeplejack."

As long as blood is the nectar of thought and the mind
                      blinks its constellations
there is more to a memory of love,
even of the slightest welcoming smile,
than to all the inconceivable loss of the world.
How practical love is.

V. The Satisfaction of Impossible Tasks

What *does* peace mean? It's not beyond us. There's just
so much debris to be carted off,
so much dust to be polished away. It's there, though,
just as we're still here under our wrinkles and luggage of fat.
"There is no unsuitable smile."*
Polishing a mountain's just too hard
when you want a definitive shine.
Peace and love are what they are,
and you have to be there, polishing, polishing. Devotion
is the question that answers can't resist.
Force ruins everything. Comets won't come when they're called.
Stars won't line up in a message and tell you what to do.
The one least fallible pleasure is, infallibly, just trust.
The impossible isn't a thing we can know.
It's unsuitable to think so.
"What does peace *mean*?" the tragic chorus pleads.
Every happy child can tell us with a smile. ■

----

*From Marianne Moore's poem "Style."

Five Complicities

for my mother, Edith Barrett Price, Christmas 1999

I.

She felt like a great, exotic, dry leaf in my arms.
I carried her up our steep back steps on the last Christmas Day of her life.
Homesick again, sleet in my bones, my mother's been dead for twenty-two years.
I savor her life, but I don't feel safe, *until*
she sets the softest trap to find me
in a place inside me I'd forgotten was still there,
a place where the past is never over and the future never runs out.
I see her, but I cannot reach her. I hurry slowly
to catch up with her smile
down in the warmest ring of my heart
where I open out onto the sky.

And there I feel her all around me in the night, her fathomless,
intimate cool hand on my brow, her smile
an epiphany of kind overlooking,
of vast forgiving beyond any ending.
Sipping champagne, kissing dark chocolates,
a Cheshire moon in winter skies, she hands me one
nylon stocking
drooping with candies, toy soldiers,
dreams of all kinds and surprises,
and welcomes me into her boudoir of stars, no brighter
than her eyes, an accomplice again
in homely joys, comfortably far and wise.

II.

What a Christmas it would be
if, as we fight off dying down the road,
with all our mysterious affections still in place,
we unaccountably succumb to feeling

quite gleefully safe, relieved, with a dire joy,
of all our worries, panics, paranoias,
of grim world history itself,
its infinite morgue of horrors,

relieved of the weight of everything,
the whole cosmos vanishing
like a film across our eyes,
everything, for us, all over. Gone.

Is that the same wild peace you felt
the morning you surprised us with your leaving?
Did you suddenly fall in love with your death,
was it like the scent of roses is to lovers,

or the sight of waists with red ribbons draped might be,
an inspiration to surrender up
the false safety of despair,
the voodoo of your nihilistic highs,

to live at last just edgewise for an instant more,
slipping through to happiness
under cover of darkness,
an accomplice in the sweet escape?

III.

Our lives are not problems we cannot solve.
Even making peace with the dread
tangles of child life, and all its sly oppressions,
is a craft to be learned. I remember my mother's
first frown at me when I wailed at tipping over
a cup of milk when I was five
and the redemption of her smile
and her advice: "Don't cry over spilt milk,"
she said, dropping a whole bottle of it
on the floor with a crashing splat.
What was *that*
miracle all about?

Is it that our friendliness with our flaws,
our unexpected patterns, our mad surprises,
teach us that love's complicity
is everything we want with the night,
with the hundred billion stars in the Milky Way,
with the forces that conceived us
in the endless blossoming of light?
We want to be as intimate
with the source of all our wonder,
as babbling toddlers are
bashfully stunned by being comprehended
when the source of all their pleasure

gives them what they want
because they asked for it.

IV.

When you died, it hurt so bad
the space you left became my anesthetic.
All that room's still left for you
and no one but you will know it.
I won't call it sobering. But it did
cause a mortal thrill in me
to think this Christmas, this most
intimate and simple fun, could be *my* last,
or one of the last four or five that I have,
not that I have an intuition that it will,
or any impending sense,

it's just that the math is working out that way.
These days are all more and more
like an intimate, dreamy warmth
too sweet to ever end
ending right before my eyes.
That's why time's the great authority on joy;
and why we measure it.
Death caught you so fast.
No one wants to be a spendthrift
and forget to notice
the ride is always about to end.

V.

For Lou Andreas-Salomé

I've had this strange and dangerous urge
to confess my desire
to rehabilitate St. Nick.

So I confess it.
Just like the Christ baby is
all babies,

the infant spirit of the Golden Rule,
of you equal me and I equal you,
and not the infant Hitler of the Inquisition,

the sneering clerk inspecting all
the documents of the naughty and nice,
ol' St. Nick is not

the greedy giver of stock tics
in Profits R Us, stuffing our stockings
till our credit cards burst

with famine and the wealth of nations.
He's just a symbol for
everything friendly in our lives,

the happy comforter, the giver of surprises,
the imp of satisfaction and all hopes met,
the spirit of daddy warmth,

bay rum, starched shirts, and big hands
in the small of your back
soothing all distress

—an imp, however, nonetheless.
Santa's not a god.
Even our culture's happiest thought

couldn't make such sweet
justice, such friendly
pleasure the holy gifts they surely are. ■

Five Epiphanies of Letting Go

Christmas 1997

I. Just Like That

Liberty from fear, that clearest happiness,
can happen just like that, fast as ice
returns to water, as water lifts itself
from weight, vaporous as luck.

You never know exactly when, but just like that the neutral world
is radical delight, chains evaporate, stains come clean,
the glue of dread is drained, long struggles fade, and hopeless goals
welcome you without restraint. Who can calculate? This sudden, free

deep breathing, after smothering in disbelief,
is nothing to expect. We can only wait alert,
so trusting of our chances never to desert us

we make room for nothing we can know
until it comes to us in wild relief like fate,
and for once, like that, we're not too late.

II. Not Fallen After All

Self-knowledge turns out to be
like blowing dust from a shell one day and finding it
all radiant pure pleasure, like fogging up a jasper globe

and rubbing it on your shirt until
the magnificent insignificance
of its details can't be missed.

Nothing in the universe is flawed. So we
are not, at heart, less than we are,
quantum misfits dirty with mortality,

in need of thumbscrews, dungeons, moral spies
to conform us to opinions that force has turned to lies.
We're not like that after all. It's not our fault we die.

Coming clean is simple as a puff of breath, a single choice
to hear our pains and truths in another's breath and voice.

III. Who First Treated You Like a Person First?

We're all curiosities, more or less,
lonely in some universal way
unique to us, isolated in our mirrors,
freaks of beauty, freaks of wealth,

freaks of fame, of gossip, or our sex;
freaks of poverty, or class, or brains,
of clothes, or teeth, or awful hair. But then,
just once, at first, we see that we are to someone else

just who we are to ourselves. We're stunned. They love us,
despite what they know of us. And fear escapes us;

there's nothing, now, we can't reveal, even privacies aren't secrets.
This is a miracle we never forget. It's in our bones, this peace

that comes with being known, this gift that let us look beneath
our fear of ourselves and gave us a life to keep living.

IV. We're So Afraid of What They'll Say

We can't help hiding.
It's cleaner than lying, our logic sneers,
like craving the noose when we're drowning.
Most of the time we are missing.

We've disappeared so well, we can't even escape,
snared by our own camouflage,
startled horribly awake, forgetting who we are,
frantic to take a chance, to jump headfirst

into the head of someone else, sick with worry
they'll step aside, drum their fingers, let us fall
into the hell of their garbage-disposal judgment calls.
Oh, wake up! Let go! They're all as scared as we are.

Listen to their fear. Let it track you down,
hear it and you'll be heard.

V. Giving Joy Away

All this worry, all this inward scheming,
all this vivisection of ourselves, our molasses longings,
our wicked little shame

of exactly how we look, all our habits of fret
that screw us down so tight our heads break off from the stress.
But that old man over there, he never worries

about being old and so close to death,
never worries as a motive or distraction;
he never worries the sleigh won't fly.

Gently, gently, he sees himself rising, lifting up and soaring,
giving and giving without worry until
he gives himself all away, like time gives away

all its sweet days. Could there be
anyone more fulfilled than he? ■

from *Five Gifts*

Christmas 1996

I. The Shadows of Pens

I was thinking of gifts
when the shadow of my pen point on the page
seemed ominous and strange with meaning

and recalled to me all the women and all the men
who had given all their breath and all their hope
just to hold up a few honest words

in the face the great
the joyless snarl
that wanted them still, so still

they would be like snow falling on snow,
all of them compressed into a white noise, so flat, so blank
it turns to vapor, soundless with the slightest heat.

I saw my pen point moving on the page
and felt in myself the lifetimes of ink
living through hands that move pens
so eyes can find thoughts
rising like words from mist across mountains.
And I saw myself as a whisper of light

in that luminous flow of shades
that moved the shadow of my pen point on the page,
saw that I was, myself, being written

by their desire to write,
those so many lives bright-gifted and destroyed.
And I couldn't help hear pens all around me

scratching out words from prisons and graves,
and I knew what I owed them—the starved, the tortured,
the failed, the hung, the far, thunderous
whisper of their ink as it flows illumined from lives into lives

—I owed them everything, even my faith, even my desire.
My life had become their gift to me, as we all are gifted

by the flow of air, of passion, of courage, of brave delight.
As I saw my pen point and its shadow
draw my life on the page before me,

I felt myself outgrow myself,
grow invisible and safe in the crowds of the defiant,
and I knew I would never write words on a page again

and feel alone, that the shadow of their will,
their refusal to be still,
would not desert me—that shadow like a burn,

like age, would never wash away in sunlight or in fire,
in the lamplight in my room, or the ash light
of a dungeon's moon . . . I was thinking of gifts.

IV. For Talia Sandra Price

—on her first Christmas

I know three gifts
no one can give you.

First, the kind of knowledge a bird needs
to trust the air with itself,
> the kind of ease that you will need
> to entrust yourself to your strength.

Second, the kind of humor the dying need
to entrust their hope to pain,
> the kind of fearlessness that you might need
> to dream yourself sane in a war.

Third, the kind of peace the self-fulfilling always need
to reject the cruel in the cause of kindness,
> the kind of dignity you will need to question yourself
> when you're burning with the certainty of right and wrong.

These the world won't give you as it tests you.
You will have to find them on your own, and as you do,
> the gift of your growth will become
> the gift that your life gives to everyone else, even to me. ■

Starlight in the Woods

for Ryan Keir Price, b. July 13, 1994

> *Yet as a wheel moves smoothly, free from jars,*
> *My will and my desire were turned by love,*
> *The love that moves the sun and other stars.*
> —Dante, *Paradiso*

Christmas 1994

There is no map to guide us through the forest,
    no homing echoes through the void,
        no comfort in the urge of data
        extruding without end or purpose.

We've looked and looked for something obvious,
    some rule to guide us,
        something that made sense of Hitler
        and his smiling mother.

And we've learned it's useless to stay confused.

The guide
is
a gift.

It wasn't hiding
in the tracklessness of chance.

It was with us all along,
    we've learned,
        with us in our arms,

in the faces of our children,
in our lovers' eyes,
before us across a table
in the voices of our friends,
in our love of rocks, and stars, and weather,
in all
mysterious affections.

How we see is what we see,
we've learned.

Effortless, I see you.
You give me ease,
an ease to follow,
a guiding clarity
in mires of distraction,
a truthfulness
beyond The Truth.

Like the absolute,
true impulse
to take a breath,
I look at you
and find my way
by just
the sight of you
—your smile
the midnight sky
holy and windy with eternities of stars. ■

Reversing the Fall

for Chris who took us there

> *I swear the earth shall surely be complete to him or her*
> *who shall be complete.*
> *The earth remains jagged and broken only to him or her*
> *who remains jagged and broken.*
> —Walt Whitman, "A Song of the Rolling Earth—No. 3"

At Canyon de Chelly,
at its infinite edge,
looking down,
a thousand feet down, overcome,
opened before its untouchable grace,
forbidden,
its visible fields, far meadows, and groves,
its terranean stream,
safe, far away,
so far away, exultantly far, that its grace
becomes our desire;
and the stories we tell to ourselves,
the lives we would live there,
our longing for dawns at the floor of the deep,
in the mind of the place, canyon walls guiding
light through the brain.
At the infinite edge, the urge is to fly,
to embrace what is seen . . . but the fall,
the mortal distinction,
the death between flesh and world.

We walked
down into de Chelly that day, actually down, descending
into desire, and
into the real canyon we'd seen,
reaching the stream, our real feet in the mud,
swifts in the air above us, sky above them,
actually there, there with our bodies,
our real nerves touching the rock, the water:
we were
what we'd desired, our brains filled with the place
and what we had made of the place, together
reversing the Fall.
At the farthest part of ourselves
we'd disappeared into de Chelly;
the distance had opened
out into that place in the self
no longer the self, but complete,
as one might glance at the morning star and know
no distance exists between eyes and light,
between light and brain,
between stars and the self's earthly night. ■

—Christmas 1983

Changing

for Marjorie Herman Rini, 1914–1980

>   " . . . *just once,*
>   *everything, only for once.*"

Icons of change, mortality,
the coming and the going,
this here and now . . . now,
there is your smiling,
your healing smile,
your serious frivolity as whimsey's sage;
in the face of evil or of pain,
your Cheshire form crusading,
adding, as you said we must,
love to the way things are.

Your presence now
diffused through time
permits no empty, grim dark
self-escaping.
The humor in death
is that it's all over,
is that it is not
its sadness to be escaped.

To escape, belong,
love change,
belong to what does not remain,
the coming and the going,
the crow noise, windshine,
gust light through the leaves,
green wind morning shade,
ripples of the muskrat,
of vanished seas on canyon stone,
the brittle valleys in the clay
leached up from rain,
your smiling, gallant toddling
 . . . love does not preserve,
it knows;
it is enough.
The humor in death
is that it's all over,
as your presence is
your smile; your gift to us
this here and now, this once
that is this Christmas almost past. ■

—Christmas 1980

Necessary Quality: A Gift

We are never poor of luxury
       while in sympathy with quality,
with craftsmanship, restraint and thrift,
       and careful durability—
the common eccentricities
       abundant in our poverties.
So, if you still believe in giving gifts,

in Christmas gifts, ingenious gifts,
in generous, genial gifts
       like bone,
your big present, then, from me this year will be
       your own most bountiful
and merry body, offered temptingly
       beneath your tree; and you

responding to this luxury
       with gracious curiosity.
A gift's sole pleasure
       is in having all its mysteries released
in use, in gratitude,
       in thoughtful Will renewed.
So if you still believe in giving gifts

release your body
from at least *one* boring truth this year
       by being so inspired, so intrigued
as to feel beneath the wrapping
       to violate appearance
by handling the goods,
       exploring

underneath your face, your wrists,
       your fingers, arms and feet,
releasing, genial to your consciousness,
       your own considerate
and confidential bone—
       so diligent, devoted,
compulsory, and lavish.

In other years,
I would have brought you tapir skulls,
       bear toes, the spines of newts,
or lizard bones—
       a million, billion lizards
and not a sloppy vertebra,
       each one fits—
to intrigue your generosity,
       to lavish you with quality,
with craftsmanship, restraint and thrift,
       and careful durability:
with beauty
       that functions
beautifully.

But this poor year,
I can only just afford our own,
       our own slow bones,
so kind, so patient,
       so presumed upon,
neglected,
       misinterpreted, and slandered:

"Skull and Cross Bones,"
       the cheapest cut of all.

Our own skulls!
　　how meanly we misuse them
those ingenious,
　　　caring functions, those
reliquaries

that still preserve
(in our Will to give,
　　　to trust, and work)
the purpose of that Confidence
　　　that caused the light
that aspired to our eyes
　　　that last silent night

that last saw God
　　complete, at last,
　　his last kind thought.

　　　　　　to make up for the missing miracles
　　　　　　beneath your trees
　　　　　　that would have come from me
　　　　　　had not our budget been
　　　　　　so restrained to thrifty luxuries ■

—Christmas 1970

Christmas License

When you come to our house this Christmas,
open the little jars.
You are free to have whatever you find:

the shadows of eagles in cellophane sacks;
a stack of arthritic rain;
        all your thoughts on a microdot;
a slab of the Sundance Sea;
        Goethe's bad breath over sensible gossip and gooseberry wine;
a primer on Mayan subjunctives;
        that wind the first morning you broke from her bed;
Long John Silver's confidence.

You are free to have whatever you find.
Our pleasure, indeed. But please,
be kind to Jesus and Jude, look for the truth,
take liberties with your mind. ■

—Christmas 1969

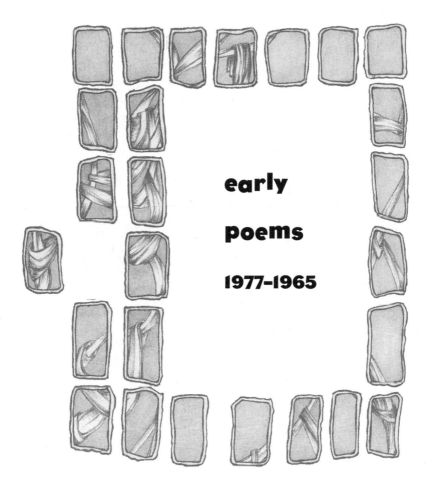

early

poems

1977–1965

The Cyclops's Garden

To whom it may concern:
as proof of my good faith,
contrition, my devout
submission to romance,
I'll simply split this eye
right down the middle,
slit it deep as my nail will go,
part the edges smartly back,
lay to rest a cherry pit inside,
then wait till spring,
till you pass by,
for it to blossom;

love is blind. ■

To Paul Klee

The sparrow sparked
the whirlpool sputtered
and as the hangman ate his supper
the swift cold tremble
of an angel's voice
was dawn by the clapping
of soft comet leaves. ■

Five Thousand Three Hundred and Twenty-Five Wolves

Sally and Gwen mount rats
over the dollhouse hearth.
Shrunken snowmen
hang by their lips.

Moonpaths, skinned
from the doddering sea,
inflame seedy stenos
with kissing sweet breath.

The Smithsonian is
the last wilderness left.
Nostalgia is not a kind burden.

The last lichen was ambushed
at dawn in Vermont.
The bounty was twenty-five cents. ■

Less Than We Bargained For

To die statuesque
for sentiment
in a village square,

limestone, sun
hewn by bare knuckles
in well-phrased
older worlds . . .

In those days, to die
was a gesture
of gentility, good breeding,
better than widows
or wheat.

Nowadays, to die
means to malfunction
and we tend to resent
shoddy goods. ■

Tempest Before Toast

Stealthy and shirtless, poking out
through a forest of clouds, first thing
retina aroused:
                            foggy leaves,
                            aerial badlands, thermal dunes,
                            vast avenues (London or Brasilia),
the huddle of mendicant sparrows
hissing.
Out there:
                        monkeys jostle for raindrops,
blue seed bananas, hot
in stoneware bowls. Oooo, the sea
steaming the windows:
                                Victorian frosts,
coffee dew on monocles, sou'westers;
Debussy inside sloshing his stew.
On the groin,
diamonds are cold,
so are orange juice drops and the sun
dazed shark-belly opal. Ah, but for the grace
of a terry cloth robe
and smoking, probing the paper.
Back here:
                        a warmth in the marrow,

like warmth in the marrow
of faded gems, heat
stored up from touching
fluorescent-onionskin chests
of countless contessas, from countless
Christmas Eve balls, regal
in genital
fox-muff dawns, steaming
under the bells
of St. Basil's. ▪

Positive Millstones*

No risks. No risks at all
—only the crossbow, abacus, usury,
and the wily Macedonian wedge
(put to good use by Bronco Nagurski
and Yalies with quilted cocks);
not the moon surely?

Why, back then
the invention of gunpowder
was as grisly to them
as the aerosol bomb is to us
and everyone had the sense to foresee
that mousetraps would, eventually,
fall into the hands of the Inquisition.

They didn't care then;
they can't afford to now.

---

*After Armstrong's great leap forward. A "positive milestone"
in the history of human inquiry.

Horizon has slipped
rare Spanish Fly,
all he way from Cathy,
into our jellied consommé'
and we bray; Titanic's curse
or Titania's, Horizon always
arises with us in her eyes.

Who *will* be the first
to plant spikes in those craters
and cover them over with papier mache?
There's not a sage alive who can bear to resist
the thought of a succulent Snipe fillet. ■

Doctor Denton was a Freudian

Monday morning:

Lubed with espresso, in Eskimo tweeds
sculpted by know-it-all, hazardous Greeks
from herringbone bought, for a song, on a lark
at a wholesome Goodwill where they still

deal in dickies, hoodwinks and spats,
snug as a fox with no shadow, a ghost
bundled up in chimney smoke and fallen leaves,
I settle over the hopes of the day, blessed,

by the chivalrous genius of nightcaps,
hot chocolate and four-poster beds, with a chilly,
taut, barebottom dawn to be warm on—warm
as the businesslike nest between us each night

where shady Lawrence,
our polar black arctic cat, is hatching a plot
to unionize hares for a franchise in fur
so birds won't fly south in the winter. ■

Lockjaws Ajar*

I said *this*
in passing.
And she told him
I'd meant *that*
emphatically instead.
Then he
got mad at him
because he didn't know
and did it anyway, even though
he had no way of knowing
that he'd done it.
And now I must explain
what she didn't say I said
for I would contradict myself
if I denied it. ■

---

*What comes of confiding banter.

Save Tsegi?*

No bruised virginity to be excused.
No hymen healed with diplomatic seals
to be opened and closed like a shutter.
No WPA to take archaic Apollo
and doctor him up, new foreskin and all.

With Tsegi there is no debate,
nothing to mitigate, exonerate
(with Jello, Tintex, or oil),
nothing to spoil, no recourse.

Eden can't be redeemed
by the Chamber of Commerce
transformed to a national park.
Of course, Tsegi, Eden, Apollo exist.
Like the ark, they are
covenants: Believe, do not touch.

No one, not even Nixon, redeems
what is cleaner that prints without fingers.
No one *can*
so condescend. ■

---

*Tsegi Canyon from nine hundred feet up. Reality,
sometimes, is a symbol for myth.

Congenital Skullduggery

Go on. You can get him.
He's a sucker. Go on,
try. Tell him the truth.
He'll be *totally* disabled.
That's right, the bushwack
—it's his one defense.
He's impervious to frontal attack.
It's a waste of time
to stalk him in a showdown
face to face.
He won't believe it.
He must catch you from behind.
Then, just ask him.
He'll be delighted,
will turn around to meet you
back to back. That's right,
tell him *exactly*
what you're going to do
—distract him,
then plunge the sword
right through your face
and stab him in the back. ■

Too Much Too Soon

Hero in a magazine
diving from a yacht:

Faded and folded
into his brain
an image in flight
he dove from the plane
trying to be
what the others forgot.

But try as he might
to be what he thought,
he couldn't forget,
nor see what he sought
before it stained his shadow. ■

Taking Notes

for Skip and Gloria

Joyous now with death around us
through the shadows we must dive,
like a hood the whole surrounds us
 . . . we are the stones to roll aside.

There is

such urgency.

Perfection

        comes and goes.

For each of us

      the future is

          quite enough,
          our gift
       and duty, but

for all of us

       metamorphosis is
       survival,
         the work of our lives
         its slow cocoon. . . .

 . . . impediments, impediments . . .
through the terror we must dive,
like a hood the whole surrounds us,
we alone eclipse our eyes. . . . ■

Only Monuments Like These

Safe at last in our garden;
married again after months
of living together like boxes of shoes;
the full moonlight
numinous bright;
each other's life
each other's oasis:
I could write for my wife in the dust
next to the man-in-the-moon she had drawn me
that "Eden
is reborn in love!"
And at the same time,
in the same light, without a seam between them,
see the searchlight sun in the clouds,
the sticky wet, dead Russian town, the white
4 x 4 beam,
and the lunatic, mute,
buried scream in her smile,
that hopeless, remote little smile
of the girl in the cap
about to be hanged
by a Nazi von Stroheim
comic book goon of a man (who had just
strung up her long, curly blond friend like a collie
not two feet away), his breath
on her nape, tightening the noose
(who had done it
so many times
he won't even watch, must drop her
and walk away as though he'd just hung out the wash)

—and the look in her eyes as she knows
that nobody knows, that nobody can,
that it's like she never was born;
as she knows
the un-
endurable
horror
of dying, unrescued, before your own mind,
is merely a second away.

This isn't strange.
It's what we bring to the world.
The garden that night: prophetic light,
that perfect, distant wish of a place come true
—Bach conducting the wind through the leaves,
tidal air warmed by the heart of the stars, shadows
created for us
by Cézanne
—it is just as real, *just as real!*
as that charnel host
those no-longer people, the breathing remains,
starved for "useful," lingering ends as exhibits, used
like monkeys or mice, vivisected; bugs smeared
into their wounds, genitals cut up like carrots
or turned inside out in slow motion,
ganglia grafted onto their brains,
who stand
in the surgical, dead, damp light of the labs,
skeletal, naked, detested,
grotesquely nude, and stare
while their pictures are being taken. ■

A "Blow-Away-Soon"

for Ian, Jacki, Jim, Rini, Marc, and Chris

It was windy green. High above us in the leaves,
the forest was the sea. We had evolved to harmonies

so vulnerable and kind, the arrangements of the pines
mirrored constellations in our brains: groves of memory

mapping childhood's times of freedom and escape.
Below the wind, the family

simple with itself—a festival of hot dogs, cedar smoke,
coffee smell, pocketknives, whittling boats. And then,

deep in afternoon, after sighting up the pines
the grand canyons of their bark, off alone in sunlight

silently we played. Without intention—drawn together,
as if composed, by the music of the place—

we cleared a circle on the forest floor;
made patterns in the needles;

gathered up an altar from the rocks;
sculpted mounds, enclosures, balanced twigs;

filled matrices with pebbles, grasses, pods, and string;
aimed shadows with instruments of stone;

and laid a path of pinecones
to infinity up the hill.

We weren't Indians or priests
or persons with a private lore,

just lovers of the day; and what we made
we gave without a gesture, leaving with the earth

a fact of our affection in a way that neither we
nor earth could understand. ■

Islands

You see it all the time
        —in the ape house
        where the hero baboon,
        in a ruin of lettuce and wet cement,
        babysits brat baboons, a shrill of oafs
        not even his own. There he sits
        pious and great, white headed,
        his jawbreaker eyes
        two-way mirrors through which
        he might be watching you think to yourself
        "What must he be thinking?"

        —or in the butcher's glass case
        with its piles of muscle disguised as meat,
        displayed in fluorescent haze, remote
        as the bony old lady, in tangerine slacks,
        with curly-gold sunset hair, half dead,
        seen through the nursing home window at night,
        stalking along on her walker,
        lost from herself inside her good looks,
        emotion disguised as exhaustion.

—or in the sweet calm of the man who said
his whole life was like
a faint smell of smoke from the attic.

You see it all the time,
that trace of more,
of surplus, superfluous truth,
what Alice saw through the tiny door: completeness
beyond anyone's reach.
That's why they call it Boot Camp Earth.
We're here to learn to be more than is needed,
to see how it feels to be less than we think
—all of us brutes with brains, however small,
our essence
is excess discounted
everywhere else but in our own eyes,
and the eyes that watch us, watching inside. ■

Loss (fragment)

A thousand years from now this hill will be
a little smaller, smoother, rounder,
and as empty of my standing here as it will be
the moment that I leave
 . . . that I should have happened at all!
those connections that produce us,
the blunders, chance encounters,
the ironies and histories other than my own,
the delicate unlikelihood
of randomness and fate
 . . . a commonplace of miracles.

A thousand years ago
this hill was bigger, rougher, sharper, and
as empty of my standing here as it will be
the moment that I leave
 . . . but one can't expect to be relieved
of one's miraculous inconsequence;
meaning forms its place.
Holes in the rocks through which time sounds,
we are shapes of being having been. Invisible,
as we must be to rocks and trees before we leave,
our absences remain: the commonplace,
direction of our lives, the view
from which to have without possession. ■

History

What of the past—
the smell of breakfast at the beach,
the dark pines, hedges, basement windows—
what happens to it
if life's as it seems: a pale
film of domes on the planet; and mind
a vapor of bubble tones, hues
alluding over the domes; and memory—
the great weight of our lives,
the substance of time—the inside of bubbles
that cannot be seen from outside? ■

Poems for Rini

Perfect Fit

You're always ahead of me.
Now you've worked yourself free
of your dearest descriptions of who you should be.
You've really washed off your ego,
the rouge of art and all that, and live,
supremely your own, released from fame,
reborn, alive as myth freed from stone.

You're always ahead of me.
I hug you, and feel the hot
small of your back on my palm.
But why are you as nude as dreams
and I'm still wearing a suit and tie?
And why is your hand
stroking the fur on my spine
if your truth hasn't disrobed me?
You're always ahead of me.

You take my hand and we dance from the dark into the light,
like oaks who've always been labeled as pines.
You have let me in
and I have grown to fit you,
clean as light fitting the sky.

Miracle Odds

I've been cornered before.
My life's been pinched by presumers.
I know how it feels to be zeroed,
to be dolled up into a target
by those who think they know who I am,
who want me to be their gossip of me.
I've spent most of my life in their candied webs.
I couldn't get out and no peace could get through.
So how is it that you
wanted me
and I wanted you
as we are,
just that,
nothing more?
How was it that you made it through?
I was ready to spend the rest of my life
wiping off people, flypaper people, like cruel cotton candy.
How is it that you
presume nothing
when everyone else
was reaching right through me, trying to get
the dream freak,
cameleon,
the yes boy they thought was behind?

Honesty Is the Wildness of the Sea

Plagues of anger choke the streets,
inflaming and distending everyone.
Hector's dead, Andromache's collapsed.
Safety was a hoax. Corpses aren't secure.

Only you for me,
        only you and I together
        stretched out in our bodies
        like myths sunbathing in the glades.
        Only we speak to each other
        as if we were the ocean.
        Anything can be said to the deep.
        Imagine being comprehended by the sea!

Anger loses its way to our house,
dazed in reefs of secrecy and trust
we have built around the wildness of the sea.

Body Life

Wearing no camouflage with you, no chains, no mail,
you let me be my body,
my body life in love with yours
—skin, nerves, muscle, bone,
no longer living armor bashed and sore
(men's bodies made for damage, to be damaged and go on);
no longer the ugliness of doubt and cheap comparison,
the panic we share at wearing the wrong
flesh fashion and skin costume;
no longer, as a man, being just a deed, a potency,
a flesh technique, an instrument, tool, a means,
a vestigial life
attached
to the back
of a penis,
clothed in body strength
to live long enough
to get the job done;
no, no longer a thing
with which
just to achieve
results,
a basting tube with half babies inside,
a builder of walls and armies as nests,
a biological dildo.

With you,
history is gone.
I know my body life
as me,
as I know myself without language, without
symbol, duty, toil, or reason,
wearing nothing because
there is nothing left
to take off,
no muscle suit, super duds, pimp fatigues,
no Darwin urge stuck on like a fig leaf,
the shame of the race under Biblical pasties,
just me
in my innocence, my exuberance
with you, free as pleasure is
unable to wear disguises, as pleasure is
incapable of guile or reason. Like flesh and self
with nothing between them,
no space for fraud, or for effect,
my body life and I, tonight, are as free as we are.

After Watching Wallace Stevens

Crickets in the books, forests looming in the shelves,
The hot green night around us like a room:
We just stone-skipped our minds
On "Sea Surface Full of Clouds,"

Just turned off the tube, just brushed our teeth,
Just took off our shoes and walked
Into the darkness that permits the stars.

Our bodies in the breezes feel as nude
As one can only feel in windy robes
—Minds like sails feel,

Like air feels rising over shoulders,
As if ideas could drape the body of the night
As dawn rays drape through early trees
The secret raiment of the day gone free.

Nausicaa

Your body startles me
moving away through the dark of the hall.
You feel to my eyes
like the breeze feels on my legs in the heat of the weeds.
    And I worship as I see
    such forms that are
    the perfection of things
    that have no perfection
—ripples, fire, fields of green,
a knee,
dogs sleep-dancing in perfect trust,
or you
walking down the hall through bedroom dusk,
your back just scratched,
Aphrodite dressed in shade,
leading me to rest
in roses, pond light,
sea wind, moss;
Venus of perfection,
philosophy disrobed,
reborn as pure anatomy
to which nothing is opposed.

Wide Awake

> *. . . I should make it plain how Love is awakened*
> *through her . . .*
>
> —Dante, "La Vita Nuova"

In love with you I'm at my best.
You are the island where the sun first rises,
the grace of right discovery, wide awake.
In you I know through love of one
one imitates the love of all,
not knowing how it feels to be
in love with the Presence of What Is,
yet doing love that way: forgiving all
expectations, allowing and letting go;
giving what you want, champion of the best,
you learn to love even who you are,
improving blindly by example,
by the gift of she who loves you
who accepts your love.

Whitman I

Duranes Lateral*

> *. . . thẹ mere fact consciousness . . ."***
> —Walt Whitman, "Beginning My Studies"

Those places that inhabit us, that are
Forms of ours as we compose them,
They are as certain people are
Matrices in which
We come upon ourselves
Evident and unaccountable.
This ditch path full of us—
Full of consciousness that's ours, full
Of consciousness that's merely
Each of us alone together
Talking to ourselves, full of consciousness
That's ours when we are the place we are
And when we're not—
It is of us
And is without us,
And that part of it that's ours
Does not belong to it,
Yet is of it
As we are
While we're there,
Our brains filling to create it,
To save it in ecstatic code:

ditch walk, heart talk,
        turtle water, water bark,

bug slide, mud shine,
mirror water, water sky,
sun leaves, living breeze,
arbor shadows, arbor screen,
wind night, snow light, winter
night glow, tunnel cold

The incantations of the code:
We are how the world is
When it is us;
And such places that we are and form
Cannot be described the same, or shared the same between us,
Even though we're there together
Rejoicing in our presence there together with the place,
But coded only in our form, in consciousness, that opening in us
Which is us and is not, which is
One and the same, which is enough,
The mere fact of which
Is enough.

---

*The Duranes Lateral is part of more than 219 miles of semirural irrigation ditches in the North and South Valleys of Albuquerque, New Mexico. Originally laid out by Spanish colonists in the seventeenth century on patterns left by Pueblo Indians, the ditches today often sustain wild areas in the heart of this burgeoning southwestern city.

**"Beginning My Studies"

Beginning my studies the first step pleas'd me so much,
The mere fact consciousness, these forms, the power of motion,
The least insect or animal, the senses, eyesight, love,
The first step I say awed me and pleas'd me so much,
I have hardly gone and hardly wished to go any farther,
But stop to loiter all the time and sing it in ecstatic songs.
—from Book I, "Inscriptions," *Leaves of Grass*

Shakespeare III: Sonnet 60

No Opposite

"Praising thy worth . . ."

Unlike the dolphin, light, or space,
love itself is cause but not effect,
not the sum of history as grace.

Time does not transfix it; it is and it is not,
and how it ends is not for circumstance
but shadows, sand, slow rocks to say.

Love is as time is, without a time that is beginning.
It comes about as if it always is,
and no amount of seeking, waiting, or deserving can make it be.

Love is not a property, it is a form of all that is,
and can't be stopped until it stops, despite its cruel hand.
Thus rending, freeing, and transforming, it is reality

that has no proof, no opposite, but must be faced
as evidence for now that praise of all is not misplaced.

Raptors at Capulin

> *. . . here all was distance.*
> *There it was breath. . . .*
> —Rainer Maria Rilke, "Duino Elegies" VIII

world through the pupil soaring in—
from Capulin's rim, volcano's crown
—as land once soared as cloud

circle of the world before us:
lava tides, ripple slid beneath the turf,
brown pastures of geometry, far utopias of snow
mirror overhead
vapor fields, windflows of terrain, thin
topographies of light, plains of everlasting blue

mind in the middle sharing sight
with vultures and the hawks,
their glide stroking land,
(as love knows what feeds it)
raptoring with their eyes
—no less, for themselves,
as victories of death, than we are
who know them from inside: Mind's angels
in their anatomy above the crown,
free of what and how we see, as we are
of what their sight has done to us,
our lungs taking traces of each other's breath,
our nerves making of each other what we can
—the ripple of their soaring, vectoring drafts
from the animal land of us there—
this consciousness between us, intimate weather
in the history of air

Heaven

for Rini, before the second operation

Itch dreams,
crazy lurk pains,
packed death settling
—everywhere we look
mad clues: bile
spilling from the car,
the threat of eyes unscrewing,
whispers scheming on the lawn
—everywhere but here:
this water dome, this perfect circle
in the center of the stone
with its groves of tomatoes and sunflower forests,
its papers and books and far corners,
its cats with their perfect hair,
and the workings at night under lamps with our pens,
the backdoor breezes, Madeira m'dear
over ice in the moonlight late before bed,
this place where we are
more who we are than we are when alone,
where we are
the place in itself, where we're known,
proven to be who we are to ourselves
through the trust we have earned
from each other—this
is heaven on earth,
our full blessing,
for nothing,
not even the worst,
makes it less.

Best Foot Forward

. . . and there is that perfect feather you found
not four yards from where we throw darts.

But what of the rest
—the illegible squalling of so many siamese souls,
the jibberish
geometrically progressed,
crescendoing
through the men's room, the president's office,
the faculty lounge,
through the office of Simon the butcher:
there's a calendar there
with photos of Venice,
Berlin, Veracruz in the rain, and Constantinople,
but Simon can't read the captions really,
or won't.

It's neo-Byzantium, mosaical!
the domino theory
all laid out on the wainscot
of Bedlam's barbershop:
rational units, arranged to equate,
grouted with rank iridescence and dandruff
depicting:
five suffragettes, Abe Lincoln,
lounging with bulldogs in bowlers puffing cigars
an hour before sunup
on *le grande jatte.*

And you and I
poke through the gala
in basic black,
our shoes
deliberately skuffed.

      (Houston beach party. Apollo XI.
      Seurat pinpointing the problem,
      but it doesn't pop. Why couldn't
      they have left us behind?!)

Moonlight Sonata

Mind land:
    full moonlight,
rising up the Jemez cliffs
like soul tide
from myth time in the canyon
when night dancers used the moon
to shape themselves with shadows like the gods;
        ice black music of the river
glistening through the gorge;
        a flood of phantom light
silvering down from Zia to Santa Ana,
moon shore full of sage and April.

To be with you on such a night,
driving into the dark,
    in exile
from the logic of the hours,
to be with you
    in Beethoven's mind
        driving through the music of the land,
        your hand on my leg, my hand on yours,
to be with you on such a night
is to be at home
        with novas,
        with the melodies of atoms,
        with the beautiful, dark
        light waves of the mind,
        formed in one life

and carried across
the canyons and flatlands of time to our lives
at home with each other
                          and the human beauty of the land
in which to love
                    is a phenomenon
                                        factual
as darkness
            giving mystery
            to light. ◼

Outtakes: *The Germ Warfare Hour*

(Pan to close-ups):

layers of priests, patriots, parrots;
mad panthers pleading with sponges;
sunflowers spinning to searchlights;
sparklers though nostrils;
vacuums sucking, succumbing to vacuums;
oak leaves plastered on patent pumps;
dragonflies flying on fire;
the sea so much saliva;
barbed wire between the stars;
barbed wire between his arms, his legs, his lungs

(Voice-over):

We have come to the block
unprepared for the shock—to a time
when nice simple people
must sharpen their kitchen knives every night
and sleep with facts
insufferably old-fashioned: ANTHRAX.
How on earth will pert Mrs. Spencer
teach those two darling daughters
to fall on the cutlery after their prayers? ■

19 Berggasse, Vienna*

It could be a place they loom silk stockings in,
mint a special summer cheese, mix sachets, or weave
wicker sockets for amputees:

19 Berggasse:
unlikely as it seems
the cockpit, womb,
backroom of a century, closet of Oz,
the rooms
of "Prof. Dr. Freud,"
occupied and civilized for forty-seven years,
open for business from "3–4," a peephole in the door.

Berggasse:
Shivering hard slick skies,
heavy with adrenaline; overcast, windy gray;
Nazi spies in trench coats
at lampposts in the street;
Marlene Dietrich in her slip
reading codes rolled out in smoke
while powdering her knees
—"rendezvous at 19 B."

Those rooms, those wishing rooms, those trying situation rooms,
like chambers puzzled in Pharaonic graves,
like catacombs, the ant hotels
dug up in sand behind two panes.
19 Berggasse:
the scene in which hysteria and pain became

magnificent and cunning;
a geode place
in which the mind could hide
and grow its own impurities
to astonishing perfections;
a dry indulgent place
where timid exhibitionists could strip, free to be
exquisitely at ease;
the nightmare house
with baby boss, id pictures on the walls,
and agonized postponements;
a place where Candida and Byron might have waltzed and wooed,
or wormed a swap with King and Sister Tut,
accepted in this neighborhood, at ease with myths,
with the customs and the contexts of these learned rooms:

a reconstructed ruin now,
a tomb of odors—smells, with their people locked away,
clinging to the taffeta, the Persian rugs,
that musk of peppermint, purses, camphor, and bay rum,
of perfume, pencilwood, old books, and inks,
and gold embossed portfolios; and somehow, too,
it smelled of rain, of sunshine, peat,
coffee, socks, waxes, and cigars,
and tiny leaves in tiny pots;

and from every surface,
in glass cabinets and on the walls,
a pantheon of all the world's lost gods, that he could find,
looked on—a totem population,
effigies, like headstones,

arranged as his horizon,
a skyline shield between himself
and his siren clientele;
Buddha, Adonis, Isis, Zeus,
Shiva, Horus, Mary, Pan
—these ultimate identities,
and hundreds more, his bodyguards and mentors,
excavated once a week
from antique dealers, like himself,
dealers in forgotten trusts,
each week this treat,
converting recompense from patient guides
to idols of his own
associations.

19 Berggasse:
Death's head gestapo knocking at the door
while outside in the night:
the lure to terror: a freezing passion,
ice white blue, flattens out the sky,
the very air out there a gleaming crust
upon which lives, like tongues, get stuck.

And I would go there now, this minute,
just to feel the pressure of his gravity,
to sense the intrigue in his tenderness for things,
his impulse to significance,
sensing always, as he did, that what is
is really more, much more than that,
something fabulously true and darkly simple.

You'd climb some stairs,
dirty wrist-gray marble with a hint of pink,
several flights perhaps,
impatient, sweaty, short of breath,
clinging to a banister that never fit your hand,
Great Freud's speakeasy just ahead.
He must have met you at the door
like a secret lover,
or a comrade in the underground,
and there you'd be—each time the first,
all lost and wrinkled, sightless and afraid,
addicted to his sexy, x-ray curiosity,
aching to be fixed, to scratch the itch again,
say those distant things again,
pick the scabs and have a look.

To enter there would be like stumbling on a stage,
a hobo from the street,
the actors, props, and action all engaged;
what else was there to do,
once you knew you that you were there,
but join the play, blend in,
become a character, belong
—until the proper cue—before you ran away,
your shadow and your odor left behind,
recorded into theories teeming with mistakes
not unlike your very own.

And near the end in '38
—as he sat there at his desk
in his great cycladic chair,

decoding lives like stricken glyphs,
still telling all-the-world
his answers were its own
—his clients were to learn
that the worst he said was true,
that living is at best
"but a round about way to death,"
for outside in the streets,
all around his rooms
the genius of his life,
his patient guides, were being solved,
removed from Vienna like fingernails
or healthy teeth, in worthless agony;
the Undermind, the icon of the times,
alive, in power, festering in the politics outside,
squeezing lives from the earth
as if it were its face,
its eyelids, closed in ecstasy,
filling up with blood
like throbbing blisters. ■

---

*From photographs taken of Freud's offices and apartment by Edmund
Engelman in March 1938.

For George Catlin and Other Heroes

> *At a mature age to make a reality*
> *Of what you have desired as a child,*
> *That is the destiny of a real human being.*
> —Nikos Kazantzakis

As hard as we tried to imagine
     we could never get it into our heads
     how people could live without drama,
what grown-ups did if they didn't play dreams,
if they didn't become their own stories.
Where did they go every day?
What could they possibly do?
     What could be worth all their doing?
We were eagles with armies,
lions in charge of the feast of the world:
     it was ours,
     —anything that was.
     We dreamed it up,
prophets and patrons of our own fates,
our lives believing us,
     making belief know,
     know us,
     far, far beyond
     the killing restraints of the Given.

It all comes true again.
Maggie and I, we were ornery nine;
there wasn't a thing worth knowing that we didn't know that day.
It was all right there in the venture:

the homely gray sorrows of thoughtful crows,
red ferns and snow,
      uphill and cold,
      off on our own—wind
dark and wet as the stone,
shadows the fragrance of steel and tomatoes,
white vulture feathers, and brown galoshes;
      winter
      and the world escaping back to the earth
      as we'd escaped—and all of a sudden,
the shock of our species upon us,
our brains so ancestral and lush with drums,
cheery, plump-peachy and blond,
tracking the heartless, saber-spined rabbits up through the pines
and down
      to the den-templed ruins of priestly bears
      —a suitable place for playing and prayer.
      Hooray!
      The spirit of who I was meant to become
      —Hard-to-be-Hunter—
came to me there. And I grew exuberant,
hard and brown—all over me
      me—fast and heroic,
      a bed sheet sculpted over my shoulders,
      a medicine robe composed,
from the tatters of costumes worn by the great:
      Captain Marvel, Lewis and Clark,
      gargantuan Vincent and Edith too,
      Gilgamesh, Lawrence, Odysseus, and Boone,
      Sinbad, Magellan,
      Lord Gordon of Khartoum.
      And George?

He was thirty-six. He didn't know it,
but he was there with us too that day,
that most American man, Catlin
of Wilkes-Barre, PA;
 in all actuality there,
 his eyes bared
 to the Mandan, Hidatsa, Hunkpapa, Oglala,
blood-brother at last
to Buck-Stalker George, On-O-Gong-A-Way's pal,
 the Great Player,
 his childhead revived,
grown up triumphant all over his life,
all dressed up all over again,
more for real
 then even he
 could dare to make believe,
as he rode those deep humping hills, the tidal soil
of the great American Desert, jangling with colors,
 medicine blues, oracular browns,
escaping the "killing restraints" of docilized people
bungled in towns
where artists must "modestly sit" and drool away
the "edge and soul" of their vision
hanging around, awaiting
the sluggish calls "of the civil."
 He'd waited so long to come true.

He knew.
 He must have known he was there.
 He *was* there, first of his kind
in the Sun Dance den of the Mandan,
invited to share, to bear witness to that
most dramatic of acts

when a soul
      must make it
      all on its vision,
must make-believe-itself strong far beyond
the killing restraints of the Given.
It all comes true again. He knew.
      As he watched them ascend,
      one by one, seized by the sun,
as they danced on the ends of its talons of light,
receiving the scars of power,
      he brushed his left cheek
      the tomahawk scar he'd earned at ten
when he played so well one of "nature's
wildest of men."
Of course he knew.
      His life had believed him.
      Prophet and patron of his own fate,
      he already was his own hero.

It all comes true again.
There I was in my garden last Sunday, planting the beets,
utterly free of their image of me,
      the escape complete,
seeing the scar still white on my knee, remembering
how I'd survived—the first time I did
      at Camp Lake Arrowhead Boy Scout Farm
      as Hard-to-be-Hunter, a star boy
      faster than fear,
losing the Snipe's men at their own game,
bashing myself down gravel hills,
so damn glad
      I bled all the way.
      Hooray!

I am the man I dreamed up to become
I am all right here in the venture,
a player without a role to be played,
no characters left to inhabit but me
        —the Given eluded,
        gargantuan still, but not blocking my view—
under my own protection at last,
everything now
new to be known
        with all the rest of my life to do.

George knew
        what to do with himself
        once he became his own hero.
He played right along,
dreamed up new dramas the hero could do,
        but their endings were over
        before he'd come true.
Vision's no match for pox and guns.
He could "snatch" none away,
        not the Mandan, Hidatsa, Hunkpapa, Oglala;
        none would arise "Phoenix-like
from the stain of the painter's pallet."
He was only their fan,
not their savior
        —the first of his kind
        to make London swoon, celebrity George
all duded up in Indian drag and cockney braves,
paving the way for Buffalo Bill. Chief
of the wild west revival,
        a preacher of paradise doomed,
        his image of them,

from the Sun Dance down
    to the dandies in top hats, coup counting in spats,
    were mugs shots merely, specimen slides
for the morgue of the race,
almost as soon as the paint was dry.
    And the world soon tired of George and his corpses.

A pauper in scars
    —his paintings, he thought,
not a National Treasure, sold off for debt
to a boiler works mogul from Philly
    —George knew what to do.
He escaped to come true, as he always had
since he first "traced the savage to his deep retreat"
when "imagination worked a charm"
and freed him to be who he was.
    He never forgot
    truth is what happens.
The Given never gives in.
Its killing restraints are only undone
by the knowledge of being beyond them.
    Old and deaf, he took off again,
ten years to himself, on one
"last ramble,"
the first of his kind
    in parts of the Amazon, Andes,
    Great Mato Grosso, Tierra del Fuego.
True to the knowledge of who he would be,
he played himself out to the end so he knew
    that making believe had come all the way true
    as the destiny of a real human being. ■

Gentleman Dada

Let me be blunt. I am not a bad man.
Why not admit it? It's no secret anymore.

I do horrible things I am proud to abhor.
It's more than my right to do what I am:
pollution, pestilence, the baiting of pets,
provisional wars; what's more, my heart beats,
my ducts secrete in the dark; I eat and maim
with the same infallible nonchalance
for which I can take no credit.
Me and my hair-trigger whimsey!
Ooo how I wish those fabulous fliers
wouldn't use nets. Yet, my wife
banks on the fact that I'm kind.
And I am, in fact, pathologically kind
to toads, to patriot roses, cuddly swine.
I know nothing of wines. I can build the sublime
in half the time. I screw
with suave compassion. I really do.

But the ants?
Can the ants understand I am not a bad man?
Can they possibly know how it feels?
Do they, for instance, record
the bushels of birdseed I've laid at their doors,
or chart the course of my shadow, build arks?
Do they wait philosophically for my spade?
I hope they do.
I hope they feel like I do
when I contemplate the news
and sigh when I come to their cities.
I hope they've taken the time
to enshrine in my backyard somewhere
a history of my deeds, some holy writ
and perhaps an idol
they curse and bite.

For better or worse, I am not a bad man.
It's more than my right to do what I am. ■

Fuzz Glut

for John Cordova

A headful   of the best   conclusions,
        a luminous, humdrumming glut,   a waste of
definitive   fuzz,   combed off the tops
        of ardently awful, lifetimes of effort   to know—
peek-a-boo, thousands   of, lifetimes   concluded
        in tough, straight to the point   immaterial   froth.

It's heady in here: seltzer numb.   Excelsior!
        The substance   of froth   is space.   And my
poor, porous   -proud brain   —O! arid, sputtering mush—
        a mess of spaces   conclusively   phrased,
published for all   to make use of   the effortless
        moments   of   usual lives,   unusually

moved   to know down behind   the trauma of clues
        that rise,   from the matter   of substance   and style,
to incite   heads,   full of room for   vacant
        conclusions,   to scavenge
for spaces   around which to
        conclude.   ■

Counting Sheep

How did it happen? When did it start?

Was it that time in New Hampshire
when Barbara's heart was so thin?
Was it in Portland that summer
I skipped and cracked my shin?
Or was it when I agreed with Paul
and dropped it all to patch up the mess in Minneapolis?
I can't recall; I've been so different ever since.

There was a moment, though, I know,
when pleasing as an aim became
too sweet an inconvenience to let go,
when it was smarter not to know the difference
between my heaven and their hell,
when I chose to decorate my soul for comfort
like a padded cell.
And now somehow my conscience
is the sum of my omissions.
And to think!
I would have died for them once
—under certain conditions.

It must have started when I came to see
that saints and honest senators
must have something up their sleeves,
that believing in tomorrow
is a tour de force to be endured
like savings bonds or slides of guided tours.

I used to think I'd sink if it weren't for that spare tire
I'd built up around my brain—but there's no security
even for the sane. After Barbara's hysterectomy
I got the gout; now, I used my phallus for a cane.

If I could just remember what I told myself that day,
play it back and lay the blame
—a time, a chance, a circumstance
would put reality to shame.

I've plagiarized my children, dissected my career,
answered all the questions I asked when I was six,
haven't meant my fun for years.
I've analyzed, apologized, taken classes at the U,
sponsored noble paper drives, creative cages at the zoo,
wooed the press with social graces
so they won't begrudge me my disgraces.

But Rip Van Winkle is my patron saint.

I wake up every morning
with lipstick on my chin,
convinced I've lived my life
in a place I've never been.

And I must be content
with projecting phantom compliments,

and settle for the peace that comes
like pantomime from proteges
who surely will remember *something*
to envy as sublime.
For nothing I'd do
would be enough
to redeem my manhood
from my successes.

I could treat myself to dirty girls,
wear wiglets drenched in prickly curls,
redress the world for millions
for mismarketing my mind;
but it's much too late to compensate
for a fate I can't believe is mine.

I will always be too old now
to die before my time. ■

Overworked

The sun or a pawn ball pecked from basalt;
the sea or a sink-full salted to gargle;
Goya's eye and Cappa's bloodshot lens;
real priorities must come first.
It is wise not to attempt reproductions.
Poems are not pretty pictures, well-wrought,
of landscapes escaping description, of nudes
not to be seen from inside. Poems are, crudely,
fingerprints of the mind, left on a certain place
at a certain time. They are meant to remind,
not define, as truth, like a hard-on, declines
the harder you try to find it. First things first.
Be what you can, then be what you can on paper. ■

Mind Jam

It happened again this morning,
that sensation toes,
of baby toes, the ends of them bursting,
blasted-out open like tiny trick cigars.
From the time I sugared my Cream of Wheat
to the last balloon of Buz Sawyer,
I felt them,
each one distinctly
—as they would feel themselves I'm sure—
seventy-five more souls explode, quite mad.
I have no idea who they were,
or where they were,
before they were here with me,
but here they were,
my brain on the blink,
tuned in from eight to nine,
bleeping the steady advance of the mass mind,
chain reacting right and left,
right within my own body.
. . . . Interesting times. ■

Being Freed

Raspberries and cream.
Superior spoons.
Cars that accelerate *uphill*.
Here I am in my garden,
excessively rested, athletic, reading Rousseau,
elaborately free not to do
exactly what I don't care to do
day after day after day.

Excellent quarts of fresh ball bearings.
Gray days.
The gulls again, the infallible waves.
I couldn't be better,
more worthy, harder at work:
extravagant labor, with effort to spare,
completed in mock-ups
implying more work.

Magnificent keyholes.
Periscoped coffins.
Bugged bidets.
Here I am in my garden,
jealous, homesick, deprived,
forced to compare my ambition,
to envy off-duty spies.

Fifty-one cards!
Always one marble, one racket, ten thousand bats and no ball!
But, curiosity must
not be confused with greed. Besides,
I'm admonished to premeditate.
Premeditate my failures? My hunger?
Be prepared? Weave baskets
—beheaded by the finish line wire,
am I?

The last in a long line of lemmings
muttered all the way home from the edge.
It has to do with King's X,
with overboard swimmers who made it to shore,
with students who hum home in the dark,
through with a test of a lifetime of testing.
School's out!
That's what's missing when you're free. ■

Notes

Introduction to *Myth Waking*

The metaphoric usefulness of the gods of the ancient Greeks may have slipped into academic backwaters and genteel obscurity, but it's never been extinguished. The old gods resonate particularly with the sensibilities of younger readers. When they first encounter Homer, the gods seem preposterously wonderful, a happy if troubling mixture of boundless power reveling in boundless folly. Students don't know what to make of them exactly, but every so often, one of the gods comes to life for someone. As if a code suddenly has been broken, the mystery of the god's contradictions reveals itself, more like a seductive scent or flavor than an idea to be analyzed and explained. Indeed, the gods still lurk beneath our charismatic bureaucratic culture of commerce and obedience. They have much to give us as we struggle to diagnose the pathologies of our way of life as well as its subtle and pragmatic moral strengths. No one would want Zeus as president, for instance, or to fall under the curse of Aphrodite in her more excessive states. Apollo would flay us all alive for the slightest transgression from his zero tolerance sense of right and wrong. And who but an idiot would hire Hermes to run the accounting department of a great corporation? And yet in the proper setting, Zeus comforts all suppliants, laughter-loving Aphrodite is the glory of creation, Apollo's mind becomes the home of ideal forms, and the myth of Hermes tells us more about honorable persuasion and adventuring into the truth than anything else I can think of.

Hermes is the genius of indirection. He knows how to win people over. It's not a trick. It's about paying attention, about the gentle field of attraction caused by an attentive being. Hermes doesn't deal in coercion. Indirection makes room; it never demands. Only force can take what it wants directly. And force destroys or taints whatever it goes after. Hermes knows the end is determined completely by the means, and that indirect means are ultimately pragmatic when it comes to following the muses or listening your way into an agreement by helping someone listen to you as you listen to them. With Hermes, it's the flow, the moving along, the revisions, the getting it right that matters. Journeys are about accumulation of time, distance, and places; and Hermes knows how to let life add up to where he wants to go.

Hermes is the guide for writers like me who follow the muses without needing to know where they're going until they get there. I had no intention of writing a personal version of *The Homeric Hymns*. At first, all I wanted was to write a poem about Hermes. I'd been drawn to him for almost two decades since I started teaching the classics in translation at the University of New Mexico University Honors Program. He was like one of those rare places you visit that transform your life by their mere existence. I was mystified by the constellation of his associations as a communicator, boundary marker, pathfinder, rescuer, truth bender, peacemaker, noble rascal. I didn't come to believe in Hermes, per se. I find it impossible to believe in any religion's supernatural beings, as beings. But Hermes was, and is, believable to me, in a way that I find uniquely unoppressive.

As a person raised in a nominally Christian household, I've had to come to terms with the reality of Jesus, for instance, as not only a lightning rod for a stupefying array of interpretations and a menacing history of religious politics of the most vicious kind, but also as a bearer of what I consider to be deep human wisdom, especially as Jesus comes to us from the Apostle Matthew. Jesus, who sees goodwill and agapé as both pragmatic and obligatory, is morally believable, in the same way that Hermes is believable as an embodiment of the best of human consciousness, with all its associated checks and balances in place keeping hubris at bay. Early on, I started to see Hermes in two ways, first, as the realization of a distinct, universal quality of human nature; and, second, as a god without dogma, as all the old Greek gods were before the Orphic reformation and its emphasis on reincarnation and retribution. The eye-opening idea that the old gods were free of dogma came to me from Robert George, a physician and classics scholar, during our many happy, fulfilling, and catalytic conversations about translation, Hellenic culture, and "the gods."

Dr. George also holds that it's not very fruitful to see ancient Greek deities as "archetypes," or deep, pan-cultural unconscious forms. He feels they are, rather, "epitomes" of pragmatic action, and states of mind, in specific circumstances. The gods serve, in other words, less as models than as guides to particular situations. Hermes is a master of changing someone's heart, of winning people over, as he did with Zeus and Apollo when his thievery and deception were found out. But it's the context of this story that makes Hermes believable within it. He was Zeus's bastard son by Maia and Hermes was determined not to be abandoned by his father. He insisted that he be allowed to take his place among the Olympians. His acceptance as a son and major god could not be taken by force or guile from the master of the universe. This rightful gift had to be given to him freely. Hermes's task was to see to it that Zeus and Apollo spontaneously accepted him. He took an indirect and oblique approach in the form of preposterous lies, high humor, sly gift giving, and feats of prowess and misdirection that were outrageous but benign enough to win them over. Who could refuse a newborn god, fresh from the cradle, able to steal divine oxen, invent the lyre, and wiggle his eyebrows so fetchingly when he fibbed?

Like Hermes's accretion of surprises and sleights of proof, the poems in this collection accumulated themselves over many drafts. I'd never suspected such mythic figures would form themselves independently in my imagination. As I accumulated the poems, the images that came to me had the feeling of found objects. I had to use them or they would disappear. Like certain places of power, such as Chaco Canyon, the myths didn't alter reality for me, or give me new ways of seeing the world, but they did show me how life is, in its full perversity and deepest joy. I had to always keep in mind, though, that the Greek myths were never meant to show anyone how to live. What did the ancient Greeks know that would allow them to put under one divine persona all those barely but profoundly associated qualities? More and more these composite stories became a part of my own lexicon of understanding. Athena, the goddess of culture and stealth in warfare, taught me about breaking the rules to win. Asclepius, the perfect physician, showed me the wisdom of death. Through Hestia, goddess of the hearth, I felt the still point more clearly than through any inspiration from Eliot or Zen teaching. Each god was telling me how deeply pertinent all forms of human wisdom are, no matter how far flung or distant, even those that undergird our culture in its current state of dilapidation.

Unburdened by dogma, but rich in metaphor and narrative, Greek religion can still be presented to modern people as useful stories and perceptions that have been liberated by the paradox of strangeness and familiarity. The gods come to us from a profound cultural distance that still foreshadows much of the contradictory nature of our present state as a civilization. This distance allows us to approach the myths of the gods not quite as literature, and not at all as gospel. They simply have a human truth about them, charged with a universal sympathy that results in feelings of intimacy and inner comprehension. It's the mixed feelings we have about Greek gods, the distance and proximity, that make them so lifelike, so difficult to grasp, and so warmly rewarding to pursue. They inevitably teach us about ourselves in ways we cannot experience without them. Who can't identify with Aphrodite in both her laughter-loving and her sinister, addictive avatars? It's the same with Artemis, the divine nine-year-old girl, heroine, loner, protector of the vulnerable, and symbol of all that should never be touched or despoiled.

Hermes attracts me so strongly, I think, because his vast complications were at once familiar to me and forebodingly mysterious. He confused me and made instant sense to me. He gave form to an astonishing association of qualities that, when connected through his personage, helped me to make more sense of the world of action and policy than I had before. Hermes is the guide of travelers and the dead, the god of businessmen, thieves, diplomats, the lover of Aphrodite, guardian of the infant Dionysus; he's a priapic god, with his traveler's hat, his phallic herms and cairns, who is the messenger of Zeus, the father of Pan, the bringer of luck, and the master of negotiation, who created reality but never could be said to actually lie, in the sense to maliciously deceive. When I found him, I realized that here was the companion I needed in my life as a poet and journalist, as an outcast of sorts by virtue of my eccentricity and shyness, and my happy life pieced together by raw luck and paths opening miraculously before me. I don't worship Hermes, but I thank him for good fortune. I believe what he represents is true.

When I first turned to Hermes as a poet in 1998, I also encountered Thelma Sargent's lyric translations of *The Homeric Hymns*. I read Ginette Paris's wonderful book *Pagan Grace*, Rafael Lopez-Pedraza's *Hermes and His Children*, Karl Kerenyi's *Hermes Guide of Souls*, Norman O. Brown's *Hermes the Thief*, E. R. Dodds's *The Greeks and the Irrational*, and Walter Burkert's classic *Greek Religion*, and anything else I could get my hands on. But without ambition to do a personal version of all the hymns, my interest was at first that of a teaching scholar. Now that all of these poems are assembled in one place, I feel an innocent disbelief that I could have spend the last four years pouring both what I know and what I never knew I was aware of into the mold of deities no one believes in anymore. For all their distance and complications, however, I find myself each morning at the end of my meditation practice thanking Hermes, Aphrodite, and Athena for the enormous good fortune I've had in their spheres of influence.

I've been well mentored in this enterprise by Bob George. He's translated all the Greek women poets and oracles, with an annotated analysis of their work. He is the author of a soon to be completed definitive two volume work on Asclepius. Bob George has read all these poems with editorial acuity, generous insight, and enthusiasm. I'm immensely grateful, as well, for the sustained interest, inspiration, and generosity of my wife, editor, and life companion, the artist Rini Price. And I would never have completed this work without the ongoing, open-minded curiosity and warm encouragement of my brother, the cartoonist, Jim Rini; my longtime fellow adventurer in the classics and other realms, poet and writer Mary Beath; and my family of old time and new time heart friends who particularly liked these poems, including the artists Allan and Gloria Graham, architect Christopher Hungerland and artist Buff Hungerland, writer and editor Elizabeth Wolf, poet and civil rights activist Denise Clegg, planner Mikki Gober, journalist Sue Vorenberg, and novelist Daniel Abraham.

—V. B. Price
Albuquerque, December 2002

Introduction to *Chaco Trilogy*

I've never been drawn so irresistibly and consistently to any place—or almost to any person—as I have to Chaco Canyon over the last twenty years. Its attraction has never weakened, my feelings have never cooled. The source of Chaco's magnetic and transformative energies remains mysterious to me. And even my poems about it seem to me at times like sand piling up around an invisible object. But Chaco's power is as undeniable to me as apparently it was to ancestral Pueblo peoples. Its spiritual gravity concentrates attention and emotion so forcefully that they undergo a metamorphosis, emerging combined as an imaginative fluidity, a mercurial richness that can adapt to anything.

When I'm in Chaco Canyon I'm there so completely that what happens to *it* happens to *me*. And even though my stamina and optimism are always tested, nothing goes wrong in Chaco; it is its own totality; it admits of nothing being out of place; what is there and what will be there is as perfect as what has been there. Even if I were to die there, it would not be an accident, a rupture in the pattern of my life; nothing would be wrong. So to be in Chaco Canyon can be wearingly hard but safe, arduous but effortless, dependable but unpredictable; it is both mortal and infinite; peaceful, chaotic, and perpetual; loved, longed for, and fulfilling.

I slip down the north road into the canyon with the same ease as I slip into a booth at lunch across from windfall friends, those whose presences alone create an atmosphere that reveals to me the possibility of my entirety. Like their voices and the maps of their minds, the canyon's life creates in me both desire and contentment. It's impossible to resist it—the character of its light and the disposition of its shadows, its cloud tones, haziness, heat, the quality of its seclusion, its suddenness and vulnerability. I feel like Sappho with the canyon and with the friends of my life. My interest is immediate, luxurious, releasing; I can't put my attention anywhere else; I can't help but feel myself unlock, revivify. I am as satisfied with them as Sappho was with "cool feet and slenderest knees."

Some places and people are our optimum habitats, our ideal conditions. We thrive with them, reviving over and over. We always return. With them, thresholds are never crossed; boundaries expand just as we try to move beyond them, carrying us with them further and further into the fullness of ourselves and one another. With metamorphosis we can never become what we're not. Only force perverts fulfillment. Parasitic force: it has nothing to do with love or Chaco Canyon.

When I first visited Chaco in 1960, it made little impression. I was studying anthropology as an undergraduate, preoccupied with the conundrums of my own culture, but still oddly curious about Pueblo life and history. I saw my share of ruins and dances, trooping through them with the usual museum fatigue that grips us when our interest is still undeveloped. Then the tragedies and inspirations of the '60s and '70s broke over us all. For me it meant poverty, depression, divorce, estrangement from beloved children, political journalism, protest and poetry, and year after year piling up between my late adolescence and my not so young adulthood.

Then one summer in my mid-thirties, I found myself for the first time completely present in Chaco Canyon. I was there with my brother-in-law and old friend Jim Rini in a weather of grief: the first of many family deaths in the climate of our minds. The canyon's directness, its harsh clarity, smoothed the matrix of our confusions. As we approached La Fajada Butte across the desert scrub on foot that afternoon, I felt myself change, literally from one step to the next. In one stride, I felt my whole self become immediately aware of my whole environment. I'd never experienced anything remotely as intense as that connection before. A deep comfort settled into me, a trusting intimacy that has never abandoned me.

It was a matter of relationship—not of me as a thing and Chaco as a thing, but of what was possible between us. In exactly the same way as I am catalyzed by certain friends, by the atmosphere of candor and acceptance that allows me to be more than I imagined or scripted, Chaco permitted me to feel it all and likewise to be felt by it in my entirety. When one feels "in entirety" one doesn't, of course, feel everything; one feels it, as a human can, all at once in shadow form, in suggestion, not as a god who could feel it all in absolute detail. But again, it's the relationship that matters. And I'm more convinced than ever, as the years go on, that it is exactly the same with places as it is with people. Some places make you uneasy, or threaten you and make you want to withdraw. Some are ephemerally pleasant, decoratively pretty, others monumental, gaspingly beautiful or intimidating. Many places simply leave you flat. They have no life for you, nothing to impart. You feel played out when you're in them, used up, or fatally bored. There is nothing more deadening or dampening than being with a person like that either, one who does not catalyze your capacity for imagination and honesty. It's the difference, say, between breakfasting with an old acquaintance who likes you and needs you but who has nothing on his mind and who causes you to have nothing on yours, the difference between that and dining, say, with a windfall friend, someone you never would have expected, someone you met and instantly felt entirely at home with, so that you became completely possible in their presence, and they in yours.

That's how Chaco was for me that first trip with my brother Jim. Its desolate beauty, the galactic slowness of its ruins—ruins of oceans, of fishes, of human beings, ruins of its seafloors and its tallest buildings, of its sky watchers and its sharks, the phantom fullness of its missing days all present in the present now—I sensed them all that day. And I felt that the Canyon understood me—my hiddenness, my desire to be as anonymous as the human lives that once inhabited the Canyon, my attraction to emptiness and to the free safety I feel in dangerous weathers.

The relationship is everything. It's as if the Canyon and I had already experienced the full history of our encounter and were living it now in recollection. This life-changing intimacy with personal landscape and personal friends is like revelation without doctrine, like the experience of mysteries without initiation. So it is not as odd as it might first seem to associate Chaco with friendship and both with the divine. Some of us need hands and warm stones and hot minds to believe. It is like that with deep friendships and intuitive connections. We know each other as if we were each other, which means we do not expect each other to be what we know, but trust each other to be anything we are.

—V. B. Price
Albuquerque, June 1998

Introduction to *Death Self**

The poems of *Death Self* were started in 1993 when V. B. Price was in his fifty-second year. Fifty-two was the age his great-grandfather, the American tragedian Lawrence Patrick Barrett, died in 1891. It was the age at which his mother, the American stage actress Edith Barrett Price, had always feared she would die. Edith Barrett, in fact, lived to the age seventy-three and died in Albuquerque after a long career on Broadway, in films, television, and on the California stage. In 1993, V. B. Price decided to shake off whatever ghost fears might be stirring in his imagination and make friends with his own death. He was helped in that happy task by Rini Price's robust recovery from cancer and by the German poet Rainer Maria Rilke's perspective on the inevitably private and unique nature of each person's death. The title *Death Self* comes from Price's intuition that what we were before we were born and what we are after we die are of the same stuff as who we are when we're alive, or at least part of the same flow or essential spectrum.

Twenty years earlier, in 1974, V. B. Price's appendix perforated. As he was being wheeled into the operating room for emergency surgery, he realized, to his astonishment, that he was completely without fear of death. This unexpected response to a potentially fatal emergency, Price reasoned gratefully, must be rooted in his conviction, gained from his father and mother, that the life experience, the universe, and the divine, were all in the realm of the good, the fair, the just, and the forgiving. In Rini Price's odyssey from multiple operations for cancer to her refusal to submit to faulty and dangerous prognoses, V. B. Price saw that making friends with one's death is really all about making friends with one's life, as it actually is.

---

*This is the original introduction to *Death Self*, which included seventeen poems by V. B. Price and reproductions of seventeen paintings by Rini Price.

Some fifteen years later in Chaco Canyon, working on a book called *Chaco Body* with photographer Kirk Gittings, Price experienced another gift of liberation in which he felt that the world, and anything that might happen in it, and to him in it, was beyond the realm of fear or worry or "wrongness."

The *Death Self* poems are recollections of encounters V. B. Price sought out with his death self, as well as of conversations he had with that part of himself, which is happier and wiser and full of more humor than he has ever been without it, without the society of his life before birth and after death.

The paintings of *Death Self* arose in Rini Price during the months that the *Death Self* poems were being written and read to her. The paintings are not responses to specific poems, and are not illustrations of them, but the process of death-self thinking, long familiar to her, released in her these images in spontaneous ways, following another near-Rilkean outpouring of twenty-seven paintings the year before, which were referred to as "the angries" until they received their more formal title from Rini's father-in law—"In Your Face"—a short time before he died.

Rini Price holds that "whatever is *is* OK because that's where you start from. It's got to be OK because that's what is. What you do with it, how you approach it, is what matters." Both Prices ascribe to the view expressed in Viktor Frankl's book *Man's Search for Meaning* that the only freedom that can never been taken away from a person is the freedom to interpret and give meaning to what is happening to them.

Death Self is Rini Price's and V. B. Price's second formal artistic collaboration in thirty-six years of marriage, the first being the book *Seven Deadly Sins*, published by La Alameda Press. Many of V. B. Price's books, however, have been designed, and their covers conceived and carried out, by Rini Price. The exhibition of these paintings and poems, along with this volume, was in process during the last weeks of the life of S. Jack Rini, Rini Price's father, beloved by his family, and a master at living, and dying, with attentiveness, generosity, and a loving good will. S. Jack was the principle investor in *Century* magazine in the early 1980s in New Mexico, a collaboration among Rini, her two siblings, Jim Rini and Jacki Fuqua, and V. B. Price.

—V. B. Price and Rini Price
Albuquerque, January 2005

Introduction to *Seven Deadly Sins*

This version of the seven deadly sins is neither a religious nor a didactic exercise. It is the result of curiosity, of an effort to learn if the seven sins of Greco-Roman and Judeo-Christian tradition could be useful to a modern pagan such as myself, a person who is involved, however haltingly and independently, in the inner battle, the psychomachia, the conflict between the evolving spirit of one's better nature and those consuming forces within one that work, like entropy, to undermine and obstruct that development.

Living in a darkening age as we do, one in which the potential for destruction and the potential for knowledge collaborate with equal power, the concept of sin, of the tendency to moral failure—to "missing the mark," as Reinhold Niebuhr translates from the "original scripture," the Greek word *hamartia*—is as applicable to the understanding of politics and history as it is to the processes of self-revelation. The seven deadly sins themselves, however, are linked by many with folklore and fundamentalism. They seem like ethical cartoons to those who first encounter them. When I became conscious of them nearly seventeen years ago, I found some hopelessly extraneous and others cruelly primitive. But they caused in me what felt like a moral tic, a faint, involuntary affinity that I couldn't shake and that made me think it might be worth my effort to try to conserve them for myself. Against the background of what seemed to be their traditional definitions, I examined each of the seven sins, using poetry as an instrument of perception, giving each a new translation that coincided to some degree with my knowledge of my own personal failings, and with my opinions about propensities to moral failure in the modern world.

Partly because of my uneasiness with institutional religions and the pious heaviness and hypocrisy associated with the idea of sin, and partly because evil is as much a matter of ridicule as it is of pain, the poems developed into what I now call mock sermons, brief comic monologues composed in the editorial and satirical third person, and cast, irreverently, as artificial sonnets. The poems are written to be declaimed.

—V. B. Price
Albuquerque, 1980